FANTASTIC CUSTOMER SERVICE INSIDE & OUT

*Experts Share Success Secrets
that Can Turn Your
Career and Business into Gold!*

Compiled by Doug Smart

James &
Brookfield
J&B
Publishers

FANTASTIC
CUSTOMER SERVICE
INSIDE & OUT

Managing Editor: Gayle Smart
Editor: Sara Kahan
Proofing Editor: Laura Johnson
Book Designer: Paula Chance
Copyright ©2002

For more information, contact:
James & Brookfield Publishers
P.O. Box 768024
Roswell, GA 30076
℗ 770-587-9784

Library of Congress Catalog Number 2002110171

ISBN: 0-9712851-3-6

10 9 8 7 6 5 4 3 2 1

CONTENTS

Go Ahead, Laugh At Work ...It Works!

by Bobbe White

*"If people don't, won't or can't laugh in the workplace,
there's something wrong in the workplace."*

— Ron Zemke,
Managing Knock Your Socks Off Service

I bought my first pair of shoes at the age of thirty-four. A poor sharecropper's daughter? Not really. You see, for the first 34 years of my life, my parents operated shoe stores. After 43 years in business, they retired and my sister and I actually had to buy shoes! As we started shoe shopping, we found out, among other things, that Dad's level of customer service was the exception rather than the norm. Sure, he and Mom had the normal pressures of running a business: inventory, personnel, budgets and bunions, but Dad had such fun with his approach to providing unique customer service that he rarely had to deal with the problems of staff and customer retention.

Heels on Wheels

Dad embraced two forms of service that became the signature of his business . . . or perhaps "footprint" is more accurate. At closing time, a common sight was the bright blue merchandise bags in every clerk's hands. Dad and staff, whether picking children up from after-school activities, heading for the tavern, or just returning home for the evening, rarely went the direct route home. I coined it "heels on wheels," more commonly known as house calls. Pumps, purses and panty hose could be delivered right to your door with no delivery fee. What a concept! Customers ate this up. Dad's response was always, "We're driving right by your house on our way home anyway; we'll just deliver it." "Right by" was a loosely used term, fortunately, with staff living in different parts of town, but nothing was too far off the beaten path.

Irvice at Your Service

Odd-sized feet were Dad's forte. His inventory of brickbats (extra wide) to canoes (really long and/or narrow) existed to accommodate even the toughest-to-fit customer. Customers with weird widths and long flippers appreciated this level of service provided by Irv. Hence, I nicknamed him "Irvice at your Service!" Interestingly enough, Dad struggles, at times, trying to recall some former customers by name, but I'd bet he could still nail their shoe size every time! The following verse sums up how powerful service can be:

Shoes are like stress when bought a little too tight,
They pinch at your sole (soul) all day and all night.
The customer always comes back when they pinch,
"Irv, can you please stretch these shoes, just a titch?"
He walks to the back, looks up to the heavens,
"My Lord, how do I turn a size six into eleven?"
So he has a joke and a smoke with the other sales folk,
And the shoe never gets on the stretcher.
He says, "Here's your shoe. I think it'll do."
She tries it and cries, "Oh Irv, that feels better!"

Mirror, Mirror, on the Wall

Like most family business owners, my parents hoped that one of their children would stay in the business of soothing soles. Dad was always quick to point out to us the important attributes of successful people, and then he would coin a phrase so we could more easily commit these gems to memory. Leaving the front-line ranks to enter management, I carried one phrase with me that I had heard repeatedly from my father, "the mirror of customer service always reflects the image of management." A classic case of a conflicting self-image, in relationship to the delivery of its customer service, is the telephone company. If only I had the resolve to survive their endless maze of menus and recorded messages. Are there any operators working at the telephone company anymore? Decisions made by management, without regard for their impact on customer service, can have a trickle-down effect, all the way to the bottom line.

Tip 1: *Set an exuberant example yourself.*

Karyn Buxman, an internationally recognized humorist, author, and speaker, has developed her company based upon the philosophy: "Humor: Make It a Habit!" Buxman has found that a grim focus may be counterproductive on the job. "Studies have shown that people having fun stick with tasks longer, particularly repetitive ones." Allowing your staff to see the humorous side of work will result in stress-free work-places. Watch as energy levels increase and blood pressures plummet. Encourage your staff to share their sense of humor with each other as well as with customers. While this can be risky at times, it can certainly recharge energy levels and diffuse frustration.

When folks have some fun at work, morale and productivity improve. The ripple effect from a high-morale environment onto co-workers and customers is powerful. Observe high morale in action and it is apparent that the senses of humor are alive and well and the level of customer service escalates. Show me a person with no skills but who has a good attitude; I'll work with that person forever. Give me a person who possesses the skills but has a lousy attitude in general and no sense of humor in particular, and we'll pray he will stay in the proverbial revolving door of employee turnover until it lets him out onto the street. Employees providing mediocre customer service cost you time, money, and customers. Employees can't afford to have a bad attitude; employers can't afford to hire a bad attitude. The exhausting efforts that go into attitude conversion are futile. Save your energy for more promising projects.

The Hypocrisy of Mediocrity

Why we tolerate mediocrity in customer service is beyond me. As consumers, we abhor poor service. The employees with mediocre attitudes aren't having much fun either. Why then, do managers station the nastiest, unhappiest, sourpusses on the front line to snarl at guests, clients, and customers? I don't get it. Apparently, most managers don't get it either. Accept it: If you don't have the right people in the right places, you'll forever be lagging behind your competition, guaranteed. Position your personnel in a job that is a good fit with their personalities. All too often, management thinks of the placement process in reverse; hire the person, fill the position, and we'll convert them. Good luck! Another hint is to think of your staff as family and remember the analogy from my mother: "A parent is only as happy as her unhappiest child." In business terms, it might be rephrased this way: "You're only as successful as your most mediocre employee." It's your baby. . . .

Great Service Doesn't Require a Great Payroll

Is poor customer service a result of long hours, low pay, or a hard floor? I don't think so. Take the volunteer at a local charity, for example. It was casual day at my office, but a lunch meeting required that I change into business attire: suit, blouse and hose, but I'd forgotten my shoes. I quickly weighed my options:

- Go home? Too far.
- Wear my loafers? Too flat.
- Salvation Army
- Goodwill

Goodwill it was. A nice volunteer, named Ima, inquired: "Are you finding everything you need?"

Me: "Do you have anything in a black pump, size 8 or 8-1/2?" My request sounded strangely familiar to me. In a New York minute, Ima had spread an array of brand name shoes before my feet . . . pre-owned.

Ima: "You know, honey, you can have four pairs of shoes and a pair of sneakers today . . . all for free!"

Me: "I need only one pair, and I can have them back in an hour!"

Ima: "But they're cute and they fit you. Just take them. It's charity!" Slightly embarrassed, I settled on a pair of Nine West, similar to a pair my sister had worn. She was right, they were cute and they did fit. Maybe I should get two pairs. I could put one in my trunk and the other under my desk. I offered a $5.00 donation to another clerk to avoid the normal checkout procedure. I was in pumps and out of time! I phoned my father that night to report my new shoe source and such service to boot. Dad inquired, "Why didn't you call your sister? She probably could have helped you out."

Me: "She wasn't home; she was out running errands. Actually, she was dropping some clothes and shoes off at the thrift shop." (Come to think of it, those just may have been her shoes!) "Ima almost had me taking two pairs of shoes. She was amazing."

Dad asked: "Did that woman used to work for me?" And to think we're using volunteer and fantastic customer service in the same sentence. A case where there's not even low pay, but no pay!

Tip 2: *Provide a healthy environment.*

Create a workplace ambience where all employees have permission to laugh at work, within the parameters of remaining professional, and you will achieve positive and exceptional customer service.

My research results are clear: many employees aren't having any fun at work. Do they not want to have fun, or are they not allowed to have fun? Are the managers providing an environment in which their employees could actually loosen up and lighten up? Recently, I administered laughter therapy to a group of community bankers. Imagine lenders laughing, chairmen chuckling, tellers tee-heeing! The release of tension from laughter was invigorating! Participants felt less stress and more energy the rest of the day. My friend, Mary Winters, said it best:

"Some environments are so toxic, even poison ivy would have a tough time thriving in them." Sadly, companies spend excessive dollars on advertising when they would be much wiser putting these dollars into providing a healthier, happier environment.

Never before have consumers had so many choices, so little loyalty, such low tolerance and high expectations. But one thing is for certain . . . they all expect fantastic service. Every day, many employees wake up, roll out, coordinate schedules, trot the dog, consider breakfast, lunch and dinner, grab the cell phone, briefcase, workout bag, the kids' backpacks, and head down the road. Then with a quick spin through the dry cleaners, gas station and Dunkin' Donuts, we expect them to rev up their customer service engines emitting cool, calm, and professional vibes. I worked with one woman who left home in a flurry, arrived at work where she removed her overcoat, and discovered, in the presence of a male colleague, that she had remembered her suit jacket, but not her blouse! They were both surprised. I believe that if customer service personnel do not possess one very valuable characteristic, we're likely to find these fine folks on the floor in a heap behind the line of fire before the 10:00 a.m. break. (No break?) This characteristic is a sense of humor. If this sounds too simple or fluffy, just try a position in customer service for five minutes without one.

Humor can be a very useful coping tool in managing stress and avoiding burn out. A regular dose of laughter reduces stress, lowers blood pressure, improves circulation, expands the lungs, exercises muscles and boosts the immune system. Research also notes that when the body produces endorphins from laughing, the body experiences an overall feeling of well-being similar to a "runners' high." In the airline industry, where customer service hasn't exactly received great grades, Southwest Airlines has become famous for their playful approach with passengers and co-workers. Their antics may hover a bit on the unusual, if not downright ridiculous. I urge you to feast on their story called "NUTS"; it's a must-read. There's a lot to be learned about the incorporation of fun and creativity into the service delivery world.

The Humor that Lurks Within . . .

U.S. Post Office: not exactly known for humor in the workplace. A customer stepped up to the counter. The lobby was filled with customers.

Clerk: "Do you want to send this regular or Priority Mail?"

Customer: "It just doesn't really make much difference, now, does it, because the last time I sent something Priority Mail, it took a week anyway, so why do you even ask?" Those of us waiting in line heard a collective gasp. So this was how postal rage happened.

Clerk: "Let me just ask you this . . . was the eagle flying up, or was it flying upside down?"

Customer: "WHAT?"

Clerk: "Well, if the eagle was flying upside down, there's a lot more drag now!"

The patrons exhaled in relief, which turned into smiles and chuckles. Never before had I had this much fun in the post office! It became apparent that the lady and the postal clerk had rapport. She was a regular customer; he had hit a hot button and uncovered a problem. You cannot do what the clerk did with every customer, but when you have rapport with a customer, you can sometimes use humor to diffuse a frustrating situation. It works well.

The next person in line had two packages to mail. Clerk: "When would you like these delivered?

Customer: "Christmas."

Clerk: "Which one?"

Customer: (Laughs . . . sort of) "Can you just stamp these boxes with 'This End Up' and 'Fragile'?"

Clerk: "Well, yes, we can, but . . . it won't do much good. Nobody reads those stamps. But if it'll make you feel better, we can stamp them."

And they say the USPS doesn't have a sense of humor!

Lightening Up in the Error Department

Any human in the workplace has made errors. That doesn't leave any of us out, now does it? Financial lending, for example, requires several trees worth of paper to produce just one loan; occasionally, something will go awry.

Tip 3: *Keep training and fun in the same sentence.*

Not that fun is why we work, but it certainly adds appeal. In every training session I conduct, I vow to add some appropriate humor. If you follow my two training rules, you will help your staff gain more from your training sessions: (1) food and (2) fun. That's it. Whoever said "adults are just babies in bigger bodies" was right.

No Place for Sissies

Fantastic customer service can be very difficult to achieve and maintain. Trainers have perused more tapes, tips, books, and seminars than you can shake a sneaker at, only to find out fantastic customer service boils down to a few ingredients: if you or your co-workers don't just love people in general, really enjoy helping them, in particular, with their quirky requests, endless needs, and demanding demeanors, please take two steps off the front line. Customer service is no place for sissies!

One bank teller borrowed a useful tool from the hospital, a pain chart. She drew her own, which consisted of a range of faces, from grin to grimace. When the teller drawer won't balance or the customers are especially testy, she'll pull out her pain chart and confer with co-workers: "Exactly what pain level do you think I'm at right NOW?" Once consensus is reached, everyone feels better and resumes his or her business.

This may sound silly, but coping tools are very individual, as is a sense of humor. Karyn Buxman explains humor this way: "Each of us has our own idea about what's funny or what moves us, but when it happens, it can be a deep release. Humor is very personal, "almost a fingerprint," Buxman says.

Service Recoveries.

Sometimes service attempts miss the mark. This is why it's important to teach personnel: (1) the customer is almost always right, and (2) service snafus require recovery techniques. Here are a couple of examples:

- Marriott bellhop, who got grease on my raincoat, then billed me $17 for dry-cleaning! Grease happens. What happens next, though, is critical. The Marriott replaced my raincoat.

- Then there was the diner who found a UFO in her root beer float. In all her wisdom, the waitress announced: "We've been looking all over for that root beer nozzle-gear!" (But what about my root beer float?) After a bit of deliberation, Steak n Shake recovered with a free dinner and dessert around the horn. Gears happen. Service recoveries aren't an option but a necessity in order to achieve excellence.

Internal Service Recovery

A healthy work environment needs an infrastructure of stress relief because, darn it, customer service is just plain brutal some days! We must teach employees realistic techniques for managing unusual situations. Timing is critical too, because opportunity for relief/release may have to wait awhile.

Drive-up bank customer: "I want to cash this check!"

Teller checks the computer and reports: "Sir, I'm not going to be able to cash this check for you today because you have a zero balance."

Customer: "You know what? I am really sick of this bank. I'm going to close my account and take all my money out of here!"

Teller responds: "Well, Sir, you've got to do what you've got to do!" The teller thinks: (Do you need some help out with all that money? Armored truck perhaps?)

Anyone in customer service knows that you can't laugh at the moment, but you need to laugh later, or you will burn out.

Customer Service, Southern Style

Kathy Kalina, a speaker and author in healthcare, managed the stress of patient care in a unique way. As a hospice nurse, Kalina utilized a customer service tool that is applicable to any industry. She says: "You

can say just about anything about anybody when you finish your statement with: "Bless his little heart," or "God love him/her," such as in the
following fill-in-the-blank exercise: He's so _____
(difficult, obnoxious, stupid), bless his little heart!" "She's so
_____(impossible, clueless, demanding), God love her!"

Now granted, these phrases have more appeal when spoken with a
gentle, Southern drawl like Kathy's, but suffice it to say that in any
accent, these two phrases help to put even the most trying customer into
proper perspective, and you will begin to see the customer in a more
pleasant, if not amusing, light.

Tip 4: *My W.E.L.L.ness philosophy:*

Work with the little things that cause you stress.
Everywhere you look funny things are happening . . .
  but you DO have to look!
Laugh at yourself . . . before others do, because others will!
Like-minded people will share your humor and your stress.
  Find a humor buddy.

In my training programs, I suggest that employees can choose their
attitude, be consistent, be attentive, make team members look good, play
and have fun. Training resembles the feeding of our family pet goldfish,
Ellie. She swims eagerly to the surface, snaps up the flakes, flips around,
and in three seconds, her recollection of where she's just been has
bubbled into oblivion. Likewise, training must be a creative, on-going,
integral part of your staff development. There are not many new-fangled
training ideas, just the basics reworked, repackaged, and reinvented over
and over again.

Providing a positive environment where outstanding customer
service can emerge could possibly be management's biggest challenge.
The results of their efforts in developing this environment will inevitably
be reflected by the quality of service delivered. Choosing to ignore the
impact that management has in this area will reduce your profit margin
to a point into which even the narrowest foot couldn't squeeze.

In customer service, it's just one normal day after another; whatever normal is! What I do know for sure, is that when you provide leadership, environment, and training, management wins, customers win, co-workers win, and the bottom line wins. Everybody wins!

References

Freiburg, Kevin and Jackie. *NUTS! Southwest Airlines' Crazy Recipe for Business and Personal Success.* Austin, Texas: Bard Press, 1996.

Buxman, Karyn, RN, MSN, CSP, CPAE. *Jest for Success.* Roswell, Georgia. James & Brookfield Publishers, 2001.

ABOUT BOBBE WHITE

*B*obbe White helps people manage stress and find balance using the tools of humor and laughter therapy. She has experienced the changes of up-sizing and down-sizing, times of sharing and parsimony, the problems associated with apathetic leadership and the sense of optimism when led by inspired management. Her approach for incorporating laughter and humor in the workplace to improve workplace performance has been covered by the New York Times, Newsweek Japan, and Family Circle. Dividing her time between her company, Try Laughter! Inc., her husband and their two children, she is constantly in the swell of life's twists and turns. At work or home, she uses laughter to combat the stress most people experience daily. When that doesn't work, she heads for the golf course, swimming pool or enlists the support of her new therapeutic tool, Sam, the beagle. Interested? Call Bobbe and let the laughter begin!*

Contact Information:
Bobbe White
Try Laughter! Inc.
1313 South 29th Street
Quincy, IL 62301
Phone/Fax: (217) 222-1852
Toll Free: (888) 836-0051
E-mail: Bobbe@TryLaughter.com
Website: www.trylaughter.com

THE EMOTIONAL LEADERSHIP SOLUTION:
Inspiring Employees to Deliver Fantastic Customer Service

by Dave Timmons

"The quality of the play cannot surpass the quality of the cast."
— Author Unknown

Have you ever seen a highly-skilled employee who seemed to care about customers but seldom exceeded customer expectations? Or the new employee who enthusiastically joined the organization six months ago, eager to serve, but now seems indifferent? Have you ever watched an employee who wanted to do the right thing for a customer, was empowered to do so, but was afraid of making a mistake or taking the risk?

These examples of missed opportunities to delight customers can be attributed to one key missing ingredient: *Leadership*. Go ahead, hire the best people you can find who truly care about customers; train the daylights out of them; give them a competitive compensation and benefit package. That's a great beginning. But please . . . don't ruin it by handing them over to a manager who cannot or will not inspire them to reach their full potential. That is not only a waste of your up-front investment, but it remains the number one killer of human potential in the workplace: *Poor Leadership!*

This chapter will focus on the critical impact leaders have on internal customers, namely employees, in their quest to deliver fantastic customer service and be the best they can be. Not all managers are cut out for this powerful and complex role of communicator, teacher, coach, cheerleader, listener, and overall customer champion. They may understand how to manage various aspects of the business, but if they cannot reach the hearts of their employees and inspire them to be their best, the customer will be short-changed and so will profits.

Emotional Leadership

"When dealing with people, remember you are not dealing with creatures of logic, but with creatures of emotion."

— Dale Carnegie

Some people get nervous when they see the word *emotional* mentioned in the same sentence as *leadership*. This reaction stems from a common belief that has been learned inside and outside the workplace. That belief can be expressed in many ways: *"You're a leader; leave your emotions at home!"* or *"Stop wearing your emotions on your sleeve!"* or *"You are too emotional to manage people!"*

I disagree! In fact, many managers fail to motivate and lead people forward because they are not emotional enough. When you think of leaders who inspire you and make you want to give your best, would you describe them as unemotional? Probably not.

My definition of emotional leadership is *achieving desired results by creating a variety of emotional connections to the hearts and minds of your followers.* Before we discuss the power of emotional leadership on the delivery of fantastic customer service, let's break this definition down into its three components:

1. *Achieving desired results* — This will always be a defining component of any type of leadership. Leaders must produce desired results or they likely won't be leaders for very long. However, results alone will not make anyone a great leader.

2. *Creating a variety of emotional connections* — Connecting

emotionally with your employees (or followers) is the cornerstone of emotional leadership. Like great actors on the screen or stage, great leaders make us *feel* something as they lead us. They find a way to connect with us on an emotional level. The real spark of *how* they connect with us is in the variety of emotions they ignite.

3. *To the hearts and minds of your followers* — The key phrase here is *hearts and minds*. We have all seen leaders who get results by connecting only with the mind and not the heart. These leaders seem to care only about the results and not the people. Since the heart is said to be the most powerful muscle in the human body, emotional leaders have learned how to engage heart power. When the heart *and* mind are inspired, you'll find happy, motivated, and productive employees.

Therefore, emotional leaders are those special people who know how to use all of their emotions to communicate and lead their employees. They make their people feel something in their hearts *and* minds by connecting with them on an emotional level. This creates the positive motion that produces the desired results.

Your Toolbox of Emotions

Imagine asking a carpenter to build a new wooden deck on your home, and you will supply the tools. The carpenter arrives with the wood and nails and you give him only a hammer to complete the task. It soon becomes painfully obvious that the carpenter cannot deliver the beautiful deck you envisioned. Why? Because he doesn't have the proper tools (i.e., a saw, tape measure, level, etc.). Even though the carpenter has a passion for building wooden decks and has the required skills and ability, he does not have the full complement of tools to do the job right. The result is under-whelming.

The same holds true for your employees. If you have hired correctly, your employees have a passion for their customers, and they have the required skills and abilities to serve them well. But you cannot build your employees up to their potential unless you, as their leader, use the full complement of tools available to you. Your emotions represent some of the most powerful and motivating tools in your toolbox. Learning to use all of them in leading and developing people is the key to emotional leadership.

Let's look at some of the items in your toolbox of emotions. The following eight emotions are available in your leadership toolbox every day. (This is not a complete list but a great starter-set.)

Anger	**Fear**
Compassion	**Humor**
Doubt	**Joy**
Enthusiasm	**Praise**

When you are charged with the responsibility of leading people, it's important to know the difference between *feeling* emotions and *showing* emotions. All of us feel these various emotions from time to time in the workplace. But it takes courage to share what you are feeling with your employees. Emotional leaders possess this courage and accept the risk of sharing their emotions. They also know how to communicate their true feelings in a way that makes a point, teaches a skill, or motivates an action.

The following illustrations show three different emotional leadership opportunities. How would you have handled these situations?

A. Michelle is the manager of Brad, who consistently pulls the team down in his customer service scores. Michelle is angry Brad isn't trying hard enough. Michelle doesn't show her emotion for fear of hurting Brad's feelings. Michelle encourages Brad but hides her feelings.

B. John has been working with Terri to exceed her sales quota for months. Terri, after considerable effort, finally breaks her sales barrier by a large amount. John feels tremendous pride in Terri's accomplishment but doesn't praise her for fear of slowing her momentum for next month. John moves past his feelings by focusing Terri on next month's goals.

C. Sandy's team has been working overtime for three weeks to correct a backlog of customer problems caused by a computer glitch. She feels the team could use a break for some fun but is afraid they'll never get ahead of the work. Sandy dismisses her true feelings and presses on as taskmaster.

These are obvious examples of leaders who were afraid of expressing their true feelings and emotions when the situation called for it. Learning how to share what you are honestly feeling with an employee or group of employees is the sign of a maturing, emotional leader. Sharing in a way that makes a point, while protecting or enhancing an employee's self-esteem, is the sign of an *effective* emotional leader.

Let's look at how you stack up in your effective use of the emotions mentioned previously. Remember, it's not only important to show a variety of emotions as you lead, but also to *connect* to the hearts *and* minds of your employees.

Your Emotional Leadership Self-Assessment

When an actor auditions for a part, you can bet the casting director's decision will be based mostly on how well the actor projects and connects emotionally with the audience.

As a leader, what if 50 percent of your performance was based on how well you used all of your emotions to connect with your employees? How would you fare if your employees played the role of casting director and rated you on your emotional leadership effectiveness?

The following self-assessment will help you determine where you are today. To keep it simple, ask yourself these 15 questions regarding emotional leadership. After answering them honestly, have the courage to ask your employees to answer the same questions about you.

Anger   **Fear**
Compassion   **Humor**
Doubt   **Joy**
Enthusiasm   **Praise**

1. Of the list above, the top three emotions that I most often show at work are: 1_____ 2_____
   3_____

2. Of the list above, the three emotions I least often demonstrate at work are: 1_____ 2_____
   3_____

3. **T or F** I visibly praise employees in one-on-one and group situations.

4. **T or F** My employees know when and why I am angry.

5. **T or F** I speak honestly about my fears and/or doubts with my employees.

6. **T or F** I show compassion toward my employees.

7. **T or F** I am direct and honest with my employees and do not withhold feelings.

8. **T or F** I regularly use humor in my interaction with employees.

9. **T or F** I can deliver tough messages to employees when appropriate.

10. **T or F** If saddened, I am not afraid to cry in front of my employees.

11. **T or F** I regularly show enthusiasm while interacting with my employees.

12. **T or F** I take a sincere interest in my employees.

13. I am most comfortable showing the emotion of _____.

14. I am least comfortable showing the emotion of _____.

15. Of the list of emotions above, I wished I demonstrated more of _____ and less of _____.

In evaluating your answers and those of your employees, look for similarities and wide gaps. What do all of you seem to agree is an effective use of your emotions? What weak spots have you discovered that need to be strengthened? When evaluating which emotions you are most comfortable or least comfortable showing, ask yourself: Why?

Digging deep to understand *why* will set you on a path of discovery that will open up new ways to improve your emotional leadership effectiveness.

Remember, the key here is to see if you are using your full complement of emotional tools every day to lead your people. The more honest and genuine leaders can be in leading emotionally, the more likely they will connect with the hearts and minds of their employees.

Improving Your Emotional Leadership Skills

If you are like most of us, you have discovered that you lead in a certain static way. You have learned leadership techniques from previous managers, coaches, teachers, and peers and adapted them to create your own leadership style. However, many of you reading this chapter want to learn ways to improve your emotional leadership effectiveness. To help you get started, here are some suggested actions that will develop the emotional side of your leadership style:

- *Do the self-assessment* — The self-assessment in this chapter will help you learn where to focus your energy to improve your leadership skills. Be honest with yourself by candidly answering these questions and requiring your employees to do the same.

- *Role-plays and peer coaching* — Ask a peer to role-play your customer service employee while you play the manager's role. Using the list of emotions, act out how you would handle different scenarios involving praise, anger, compassion, humor, honesty, etc., with your employee. Don't be afraid to exaggerate your emotions. Ask your peer for feedback on your effectiveness.

- *Take an acting or storytelling / theater class* — Search your local performing arts center or community theater for introductory classes in acting and/or storytelling. Why? Emotional leadership depends on your ability to connect with your people. These classes show you how to connect through drama, stories, and trying new communication styles. And it's fun!

- *Become a kid again* — We know how to honestly express our multitude of emotions because we were once children. As adults we've been taught to suppress many of our emotions. Since the workplace can be stressful and serious, find ways to bring out the kid in you and your employees through campaigns, creative meetings, and team-building activities. This is a great way to connect with people and have fun in the process.

- *Observe great leaders and coaches* — While this is an obvious action to take, pay particular attention to the emotions great leaders and coaches ignite in their people. What do their followers *feel* and why? How do their feelings translate into desired results?

Emotional Leadership Opportunities in the Workplace

There are many areas in an organization where an emotional leader can greatly impact customer service through heartfelt connectivity with employees. If you have the courage to try something new, below are three areas where you can begin immediately.

Hiring New Employees / New Employee Orientation

If you are a leader who depends on newly-hired employees as part of your team, you must become visible and involved in the hiring and orientation process. What better way to begin the caring, nurturing, and connection process than to invest in a new employee's first impression of the organization? This is also a perfect opportunity to demonstrate the myriad of emotions in your leadership toolbox while focusing on customer service. Here are a few actions to consider:

- Participate in the interview process when possible. Challenge yourself to use every appropriate emotion in your toolbox when interviewing new employees. Place particular emphasis on care and concern for the employee and passion for taking care of customers.

- Offer to speak to every new group of employees during their first day of orientation. Really dramatize your organization's zeal for customer service. Tell customer service stories and highlight some of your organization's service heroes. Discuss the system used to measure customer satisfaction.

- Stay in touch with your new employees from day one of orientation through new-hire training. Answer their questions along the way and make them feel wanted and needed. Treat them like team members before they ever report to your team.

Daily Coaching and People Development

One of the most unheralded benefits of being a leader of people is making a difference in someone's life every day. Sometimes it is a series of small differences and other times it is a life-changing difference. The role of *coach* is a very serious and coveted responsibility for the emotional leader.

Whether it's one-on-one or group coaching, you have the opportunity to use your full toolbox of emotions to develop your people. When you think of some of the most successful athletic coaches, you will find many different types of personalities. But one thing they have in common is the love of teaching and developing their teams to be their best. And, they will use whatever emotional tool and teaching method necessary to bring out the best in their team members.

We can learn many effective behaviors from great coaches. The following represents some of these lessons:

- They really know their people. They know their backgrounds and their family situations. They know their interests and their motivators. They care.

- They are brutally honest and timely with their feedback. They passionately give praise and criticism with the same objective: To build up and not to tear down.

- They are constantly trying new things to gain an edge. They take risks.

- They know their customers and what it will take to exceed expectations, and they set the bar high.

- They will not tolerate *individualism* over *team.*

- They are proud of their team members and will jump to defend them as if they were family.

Listening (and Proving It)

I have met thousands of bright, educated leaders in my 25-plus years of business experience, but not one of them majored or minored in *Listening*. In fact, only a few have taken a formal class to improve their listening skills. Yet the power of a leader's ability to listen cannot be understated. Listening conveys respect, yields solutions, clarifies communication, influences decisions, and fosters new ideas.

It is nearly impossible for a leader who has poor listening skills to connect with and inspire employees. We've all heard the definition that *listening is **not** waiting for your turn to talk.* Good listeners have learned that they must block all other thoughts and interruptions from their minds and focus on the person speaking. They've also learned to listen for *feelings* and not just for words. Great listeners make it a habit to demonstrate their listening skills by giving a brief summary of what they've just heard and asking: "Did I hear you correctly?" or "Is that what you're saying?"

Here are some great listening opportunities to enhance your emotional leadership abilities and improve customer service:

- *Listening to Customers* — Find more ways to listen to customers directly, such as customer focus groups, shadowing a customer service representative, listening to phone calls, and randomly contacting customers to ask about service. Remember to share what you learn with your employees.

- *Listening to Employees While Coaching* — Resist the tendency to tell employees what they did poorly or well after listening to a customer interaction. Instead, let employees first tell you what they thought of their performance (good and bad) and what they would do to improve. Add your feedback when they are finished.

- *Listening to Employees' Ideas* — Unleash the plethora of ideas from your employees by giving them a specific customer topic or issue to solve. However, if you ask, you must listen by responding to each idea. Reward the ideas you can implement and celebrate the idea generation of those that cannot be implemented.

- *Listening to Employee Issues and Interests* — Take special care and time to listen to employee concerns and issues. Do the same in listening and learning about employee interests. These are areas where great leaders separate themselves from average leaders. This is where you really show you care about your employees as people. Remember, if you ask for this type of information, you must demonstrate you were listening by restating what they told you and remembering it weeks later. (Take notes if necessary.)

Unleashing Your Leadership Brilliance

"Our dreams can come true if we have the courage to pursue them."
— Walt Disney

As you read this chapter, believe it was written with you in mind.

Your love and passion for outstanding customer service should be surpassed only by your love and commitment to your people.

Because you are human, you already have the full complement of emotional tools inside of you, waiting to be activated. To begin unleashing your leadership brilliance, be authentic and trust your instincts. Try the activities mentioned in this chapter. Above all, be *real* in communicating how you feel and what you want from your employees in your mutual quest to deliver fantastic customer service.

Ralph Waldo Emerson said: *"What lies behind us and what lies in front of us, pales in significance to what lies within us."* You cannot change the past or predict the future, but you can find what lies within you to become the best emotional leader you can be. Find it, act on it, and you will change the world.

ABOUT DAVE TIMMONS

Dave Timmons works with organizations to develop Extreme Leaders who inspire excellence and a winning mindset in the marketplace. His passion is helping good managers find their courage to become great leaders. Dave's Extreme Leadership programs help all levels of managers learn to lead with heart (fearlessness), mind (action), and soul (emotion) in order to inspire others to performance excellence. Dave spent 25 years with two Fortune 100 banks, leading teams from 10 to 7500 employees to record sales and service performance. His leadership expertise is in sales, customer service, process improvement, and personal growth. His Extreme Leadership programs have inspired thousands of managers from coast to coast with clients such as Bank of America, Circuit City Stores, AmSouth Bank, and Suncoast Human Resource Management Association. Dave is a professional member of the National Speakers Association.

Contact Information:
Dave Timmons
Extreme Leadership Solutions
14910 N. Dale Mabry Highway
P.O. Box 340025
Tampa, FL 33694-0025
Phone: (813) 792-9829
Fax: (813) 792-9810
E-mail: Dave@DaveTimmons.com
Website: www.DaveTimmons.com

TUNE UP YOUR BUSINESS VOICE —TURN ON YOUR CUSTOMERS

by Cathy Emma

"There is no index of character so sure as the voice"
— Benjamin Disraeli

How much value do you place on your speaking voice? If you were to *lose* your voice permanently, what would it cost you? Imagine how difficult it would be to communicate with customers, suppliers, and co-workers without the use of your voice. Recent studies have revealed that at least one in four working Americans would find it impossible to pursue the profession of their choice, should their speaking voices become permanently disabled. This information makes a very strong statement concerning the role of voice and speech in today's business world. An effective speaking voice is your most important communication tool, and how you use it is especially critical when it comes to customer service. Of all the things we do naturally, like walking or breathing, the way we speak is the one natural process we most often take for granted. Never underestimate the power of your voice. Good *business* and good *speaking* make a dynamic duo for success!

Is it possible that you could be turning off your customers by the sound of your voice? Poor speaking habits and a weak voice can have an adverse effect on relationships and can be very costly in business. Your voice has the power to instantly reach out and connect with people. It can direct people toward you or turn them away. When interacting with customers, your voice can be a strong motivating factor in helping them decide whether or not they will do business with you. The way you express yourself through your language serves as your identity, just like your business card. It reveals volumes about you.

An effective voice and speaking style will vastly improve your ability to express yourself with credibility and will give you the power to be clear, precise, and right on target. Making a strong first impression is a key component in developing lasting customer relationships, and having excellent verbal skills will get you off to a good start with customers. They will want to hear more of what you have to say because your voice and words have immediately influenced them in a powerful and positive way. Developing an effective and healthy speaking voice is a wise choice for all business professionals and will result in greater customer satisfaction.

Voice Quality — the Human Factor

In today's highly advanced world of technology, communication is available in many forms, but the component of communication that remains the same is the spoken word. The *human* factor is the voice. It reflects your psychological and emotional state of mind. If you are not feeling well, or are upset in any way, it will be heard in the sound of your voice. Maintaining good physical and mental health is critical to having strong and resilient speaking abilities. The sound and quality of your voice establish the tone of your relationship with customers. A dull and uninteresting monotone voice could convey the impression that you lack enthusiasm and sincerity, and your credibility and effectiveness might be questioned. Speaking with a warm and friendly voice filled with energy and enthusiasm will express your willingness to listen and understand. You immediately become the business voice that is genuinely concerned and interested in servicing people. You have characterized yourself as a confident, well balanced, intelligent individual who *sounds* like you mean business, and you maximize your role as the voice of *trust!*

Getting the Stress out of Your Voice and Speech

Stress can have a marked influence on voice quality, speech rate, and language usage, resulting in a diminished professional image in the workplace. Being stressed can affect your overall communication impact with customers. The human factor must have balance, so it is important to understand that acting out of tension and pressure at work will lower your competence and effectiveness, and it can be very costly. Controlling your nerves will control your speech!

If you are finding it difficult to sound positive and friendly when dealing with customers, you may want to pay closer attention to the balance in your own life. Learning to spot the sources of your stress is vital to your communication abilities. Staying cool and centered is vital in customer service and is directly connected to your earning potential. Customers care about being listened to and treated with respect. Without respectful treatment, they will take their business elsewhere, so it is imperative that you keep your speaking style consistent with a professional image at all times. Realize that your voice is a tool that you carry with you wherever you go. It is a part of your physical body and is affected by your environment and all of your emotions. Allowing stress to disturb the sound of your voice or to influence your choice of words could make or break a customer connection and could even cost you a career. A curt word or any type of defensive tone is an instant turn off. You cannot retrieve your words, so choose them wisely, and never allow your tone of voice to broadcast your inner tension. Even the slightest hint of emotional insecurity can turn a friendly customer into a difficult and irate one.

The Telephone Voice

Many transactions with customers are done completely by phone without any personal contact. Your voice and the way you express yourself through your speech now become your second face. The entire responsibility of the impression you make on the customer is dependent upon the way that you sound. On the phone you are seen only through your speech, without the use of body language or facial expressions. Getting your messages across will require a dynamic vocal charisma, and therefore your words and the sound of your voice should convey a warm, friendly smile and a firm handshake. An unpleasant voice, lack of clarity, or poor grammar and enunciation will have a customer noticing these qualities, instead of listening to what you have to say. An effective telephone voice should be cheerful and interesting, conveying confidence and control. Being prepared with your best professional sounding voice will serve you well when speaking with customers on the phone.

5 Easy Tips for Your Telephone Voice

1. Smile, and your speech is automatically energized and will convey a pleasant and cooperative attitude.

2. Good posture will inject more enthusiasm into your voice. Sitting up straight will make you sound better.

3. Be an attentive listener so you can understand your customer's needs.

4. Avoid being distracted by others. Stay focused on your call.

5. Be courteous at all times, and remain professional.

Evaluate Your Voice Personality

The best way to fully grasp how you sound to others is to hear yourself on a tape recorder. In this way, you can analyze the sound of your voice and any conscious or unconscious speaking habits that you may have accumulated over a long period of time. Once you identify your vocal strengths and weaknesses, you can then begin to work on the areas that need improvement. Recording yourself in both business and casual settings is the best way to hear what you sound like to others. A small tape recorder placed where you cannot see it is a good technique to use. In this way, you will be more relaxed and comfortable with your own words. Another method is to speak directly into a recorder and talk about something that is familiar and interesting to you. Keep talking until you feel completely relaxed and are sounding like yourself without any self consciousness. Fifteen minutes will usually give you a good sampling of what you sound like to others.

After recording, you should listen attentively and make careful constructive observations about your voice. Do you like what you hear, and what do you think you can improve on? Write down your reactions, and get the opinions of trusted colleagues and friends to listen and help evaluate your voice. When you have done a complete analysis of your recording and have identified exactly what you want to change and improve in your speaking style, you will be able to start a daily program of listening and correcting.

What to Listen For After Recording

- Do I sound friendly and enthusiastic, or dull and monotonous?
- Is my speaking pace too fast or too slow?
- Am I too loud or too soft?
- Are my words clear and easy to understand?
- Do I mispronounce words or use incorrect grammar?
- Do I have a heavy regional or foreign accent?
- Do I use empty words like "uhms" or "ahs"?
- Do I clear my throat frequently when I speak?
- Do I sound professional and trustworthy?

Having a greater awareness of what you sound like is the first step to improving your voice. When you know what to listen for, it is much easier to polish and correct those tricky little verbal habits and mannerisms. Continuing to record yourself is the most valuable way to make your changes become permanent. Just be patient with yourself and be consistent with your practice. Remember that most of us were never taught to speak effectively. Our speech habits are learned behaviors which we received from our parents or the people who raised us as children. Our adult vocal behaviors have become acquired and reinforced over a long period of time, and we frequently take them for granted, not realizing that they could be a barrier to our success in life. It takes time to change old habits, but the good news is that all learned behavior can be changed for the better! Listen and practice daily.

Many business professionals are intelligent and highly talented people, but the way they talk undermines their progress. They have speech habits and mannerisms that are shared by many other people who have not been trained to pay attention to their speaking styles. Just a little extra knowledge and a few small changes can pay big dividends. Listen and learn, and if you think you need a voice coach, by all means find a good one. Replacing old speech habits with new verbal behavior can bring you great communication advantages. As you increase your vocal knowledge and stay motivated to improving your speech, you will find yourself gaining a compelling voice personality that attracts more customers and brings you success!

Listening to Your Customers' Voices

"If speaking is silver, then listening is gold."
— Turkish Proverb

Speaking more effectively will stimulate your ability to become a better listener. When you tap into a new way of speaking and self-expression, you begin to listen more closely to the voices and speaking styles of other people. By expanding your listening ability, you comprehend your customers' needs in a broader and more appreciative sense. An attitude of cooperation develops on both sides and creates a friendly atmosphere. Trust continues to build as you continue to take ownership of your communication skills. Speaking and listening with equal competency are confidence builders for all parties, where customer satisfaction reigns!

Music to Their Ears

Consider your voice as a musical instrument. This thought will help you give more attention to the way that you speak. We know that a musical instrument has to be fine tuned, maintained and well cared for. If you want your speech to be music to the ears of everyone who hears you, you will have to remember (as with all musical instruments) that you have to practice to become skilled. What you get out of it all depends on how you play it, in tune or out of tune. Yes, practice does make perfect. Your customers will appreciate your pleasant sounding voice and the friendly words that you convey to them. They will be much more inclined to listen, trust, and want to do business with you. Once you are aware of keeping your speaking style in tune and professional at all times, you will find your customers paying closer attention to what you have to say. Care for your voice just as you would care for a beautiful grand piano, a violin, a guitar, or any other musical instrument. Keep it fine tuned, and it will be at your command at all times, ready to serve you and your customers!

A One-Word Plan to Keep Your Business Voice in Tune
M U S I C

M Make yourself healthy with a great fitness program. A healthy voice needs a healthy body and a stress-free mind.

U Understand what you sound like to others by recording yourself and evaluating your speech. Listen carefully, and correct the areas that need improvement. Practice!

S Stay enthusiastic and smile whenever you speak. The energy will come through your voice and words.

I Increase your vocabulary and watch your grammar. You will sound confident and very professional.

C Courtesy counts. Your words cannot be retrieved. Choose them wisely and you will benefit.

As was stated earlier, the way you express yourself through your language identifies who you are, just like your business card. How you speak is your connection to everyone who hears you. It can attract or repel. A friendly and enthusiastic way of speaking gains the respect and trust of listeners. Your voice is your fortune and can carry you to great heights. Honor it, and use it well. Tune up your business voice, and you will definitely turn on your customers!

ABOUT CATHY EMMA

*C*athy Emma's ability to motivate and educate in the field of communi- *cation skills started with her first career as an elementary school teacher in Chicago. Her passion for quality speech and voice has led to a successful, wide-ranging career that has included musical entertainer, actress, songwriter, speaker, voice/speech communications skills trainer and author. As a multi-faceted communication expert, Cathy uses her expertise and skills to deliver dynamic keynote speeches, workshops and training sessions that provide solutions to verbal communication and pres- entation challenges. She has written and produced two songs and her audio program, Voice Personality, is used by executives, employees, students and organizations in their training programs for improving communication and telephone skills. Cathy's customized programs energize, educate and enter- tain. She holds a Bachelor of Education Degree from Chicago Teachers College and did advanced studies in Music and Communication Arts at Roosevelt University in Chicago. Cathy was featured in the "2001 Who's Who in Business" by Today's Arizona Woman.*

Contact information:
Cathy Emma
Voice Power In Business
E-mail: cathy@cathyemma.com
Website: www.cathyemma.com

LEADERSHIP: SOWING AND SERVING

by Denise Bennett

"He who sows sparingly will also reap sparingly, and he who sows bountifully will also reap bountifully."

— 2 Corinthians: 9:6

It's one of the oldest proverbs in the world and a great model for leadership and customer service, particularly in today's economically perilous times. This admonition applies to every situation and every type of company, including small businesses, major corporations, churches, and non-profit organizations, as well as to our personal and professional lives.

Let's take a closer look at this theory of sowing and reaping. What is the main ingredient in the successful operation of *any* organization? Not surprising to any of us, it is the ability to generate revenue! Leadership and sowing seeds are synonymous with revenue generation and are the core ingredients of fantastic customer service. Let's explore this idea and apply it to your company.

When you flip on the light switches around your home or office, the ceiling lights begin to shine brightly and radiate from the top of the room. So does leadership. Leadership and the core values that affect customer service begin at the top of any business, organization, faith body, or family, not at the bottom. The seeds that you sow as a leader take root in your employees, and the quality of your customer service is the end product. The end product or the bottom line is reflected on the balance sheet and income statement. It's a great idea to chart the flow of this concept.

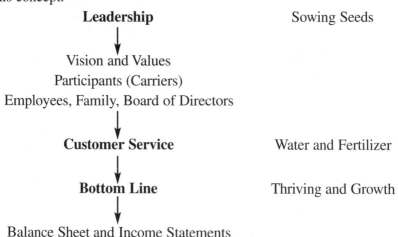

Leadership   Sowing Seeds

Vision and Values
Participants (Carriers)
Employees, Family, Board of Directors

Customer Service   Water and Fertilizer

Bottom Line   Thriving and Growth

Balance Sheet and Income Statements

Leaders must possess a *vision*. Being able to articulate that vision to the sales force is crucial to the quality of customer service in daily operations. If your bottom line is less than adequate, take a closer look at your customer service. Any flaws in your customer service ultimately affect the company's ability to generate revenue and increase sales. Sales and revenue are a reflection of your customer service. If your customer service is floundering, then focus on the participants or the "carriers." These are the persons responsible on a day-to-day basis for carrying out the vision and serving the needs of your customers and potential clients. If that service it not thriving, then the visions and values have not been sown bountifully from the leader. When there is an apparent breakdown in this process, the flowchart must be rebuilt.

Sowing seeds and serving require that the leader, CEO, CFO, sales manager, pastor or head honcho articulate the vision and sow seeds of integrity, humility, patience, honesty, and any other qualities to be transferred to the next level of management. Now, you can't transfer any quality as a leader that you can't or don't want to model yourself. If your employees constantly see you exhibit dishonesty, then don't think for a moment that they are committed to being honest with the customers they serve. If your employees observe a leader as being selfish and always involved in self-serving activities, then they certainly won't see the need to humble themselves or give of themselves willingly.

People in general have to be held accountable for their actions. Leaders have to inspect what they expect. When accountability and inspections are lacking, so is the quality of customer service rendered to clients, thereby impacting revenue generation. Once a leader sows his or her vision, it has to be nurtured. Now it's time to apply water and fertilizer. When we're dealing with employees and associates, some of them need much more water and fertilizer than others. The water and fertilizer stage is the consistent coaching, modeling, and partnering activities that lead to the survival of any organization. As a leader in your company, do you coach and observe consistently? To coach others, your employees must receive constructive information that will ultimately result in their personal and professional growth as well as in that of the company. People, in general, want to do their jobs well, but often they need to be shown how. Consistent coaching and sowing positive seeds will yield the flourishing crops that all of us are seeking.

If you sow your knowledge and experience sparingly, so will the secondary levels of management. This causes a trickle-down effect, thus negatively impacting the quality of your customer service. If you're expecting a good harvest, then you must first plant a quality seed, water it, and fertilize it.

For any of you who have planted flowers, a garden, or a crop on a farm, you know that in order to have a quality product, you must do some weeding and pruning. We will refer to the weeding and pruning as "constructive feedback." Constructive feedback sows seeds of wisdom and future greatness into folks who have promise. Again, feedback begins with the leader. The quality of the customer service that is provided to your clients is a result of the constructive feedback that has been provided to the carriers. Think about the leaders in your life who have "weeded and pruned" you over the years. They genuinely cared about you and were interested in your wellbeing and growth. If our parents, teachers, and other influential adults had not chastised us, we would still possess some of the same undesirable little habits we had as children. Corporate America is no different. When we observe bad habits and allow them to continue without coaching properly, providing constructive feedback, and modeling the desired behavior, we're negatively impacting our customer service, with the result ultimately impacting our bottom lines.

Leaders who do not have the ability to coach and provide constructive feedback typically hire folks just like them. This practice cripples an organization as everyone goes through his or her daily routine with a false sense that everything is wonderful. If you are responsible for a sales team, an organization, a congregation, or a family, and you consistently refuse to provide constructive coaching, or you pretend that you don't see what's transpiring in your surroundings, you really don't have your associates' best interests at heart. If you truly want to add value to their growth and see them succeed, then you owe it to them to provide constructive coaching and feedback. The leader creates an atmosphere in which coaching and feedback are honored. This brings to mind a question that was asked in a sales seminar: Do you perceive constructive feedback as a gift? Think back to your most recent constructive feedback. Maybe it wasn't what you wanted to hear, but it was probably what you needed to hear. When leaders lovingly provide constructive feedback, they are sowing seeds of love, wisdom, caring and promise in someone else's life. They are sowing seeds of greatness. These seeds spread and radiate from the customer service that we provide. The result is that our balance sheets and income statements flourish while the leader's vision shines through.

Your customer service will ultimately be measured by the leadership that flows down through the ranks of management. When we give of our time, talent, resources, and experience, it may appear that we're sowing sparingly, but over a period of time, cultivation yields bountiful crops and fruit and spreads throughout our organizations and the lives that we influence. Time spent cultivating the growth of the carriers of our vision is far more valuable than time centered on ourselves.

If you surveyed your customer base, how would they rank your service: good or excellent? In a tough economy, potential customers are hesitant to pay for merely good service. Many companies will provide good service. Sowing seeds and serving breed *excellence*. As leaders and influencers, let's ensure that whatever is shining down from our ceiling is what we want to be reflected on our bottom line!

ABOUT DENISE BENNETT

For over 25 years, Denise Bennett's goal has been to elevate banking professionals and clients to excel through leadership modeling. Her sales and leadership skills were shaped while working in various aspects of banking, including commercial, business, consumer and mortgage, community development, lending, and serving "Private Banking" clientele. From that practical, hands-on foundation, she launched a successful professional speaking and financial executive coaching company. Coaching Visions, LLC, is a dynamic resource designed to generate revenue by arming leaders with the tools necessary to make their financial vision a reality. Denise utilizes her leadership skills with positions on boards of directors for the Greater Raleigh Chamber of Commerce Executive Board, First Citizens Bank, Triangle Urban League and The Cardinal Club. She stays current with memberships in the National Speakers Association, NSA/Carolinas Speakers Association, and Raleigh Professional Women's Forum.

Contact Information:
Denise S. Bennett, President & CEO
Coaching Visions, LLC
6300-138 Creedmoor Road, #330
Raleigh, NC 27612
Phone: (919) 783-6470
Fax: (919) 783-7663
E-mail: dsb@coachingvisions.net
Website: www.coachingvisions.net

Body Honesty
in Customer Service:
Understanding Deception & Credibility Cues

by Patti Wood, CSP

Answer these questions to test your skill in being able to spot a liar or in being able to look credible. Take this quiz before you read the next chapter. Answers are at the end of the chapter.

Spot a Liar Multiple Choice:

1. A liar
   a. will answer questions quickly and give longer answers.
   b. will spend less time gesturing.
   c. will have longer pauses and shorter answers.

2. You can tell when someone is lying most accurately by reading
   a. facial expressions.
   b. the body.
   c. the eyes.

Look Credible Multiple Choice:

3. The best way to look honest with your body language is to
   a. be relaxed.
   b. hold a steady posture without a lot of extraneous movement.
   c. match your body language to whatever you are saying.

4. To show truthfulness when giving a presentation, hold your hands

    a. loosely at your sides or with one hand in your pocket.

    b. clasped loosely in front of you.

    c. palms open.

5. Which of the following actions would make you look more honest?

    a. Leaning toward the interviewer.

    b. Leaning back, relaxed, with your hands clasped behind your head.

    c. Wearing a suit and tie and sitting behind a desk.

6. What should you do with your mouth if you want to hide the truth?

    a. Hold it still.

    b. Maintain a slight small smile.

    c. Be careful of pursing or licking your lips.

Body Honesty

In the most important interviews of their careers, Gary Condit sucked in his lips and stuck out his tongue, Bill Clinton touched his nose about every four minutes and Enron's Ken Lay over-acted and was over-confident. In these public moments, each of these men displayed non-verbal cues of deception. They lost their credibility.

In politics and public relations, losing credibility can be disastrous. The same is true in customer service. What can be learned from the mistakes of these public figures? Can you spot a liar? And even more importantly, do you know how to avoid sending out the wrong signals?

Customers are watching you for nonverbal cues as well as listening to the words you say. If you tell a customer that you can deliver in three months and swipe your tongue across your lips, she may believe on a subconscious level that you're not being completely honest. When your front-counter employee smiles and sarcastically tells your customer he's "so sorry" the customer is upset, the words are meaningless.

Trust is a crucial ingredient in business dealings. Customers need to trust that you will be honest with them. If a customer believes that a car salesman is trying to sell a lemon or that the computer help desk is lying about the need to upgrade to their new software, that customer will take his or her business elsewhere.

There are up to 10,000 nonverbal cues packed in every minute of interaction. When someone is not telling the truth, their nonverbal behavior speaks volumes. Eyes, head, voice and hands leak out cues of withholding and deception or cues that can establish credibility.

Nonverbal communication is the way the subconscious mind speaks. No matter how much you want to control it, your nonverbal behavior gives clues to how you are truly feeling. Body language cues are undeniable although the underlying motivation and the interpretation can vary. Therefore you need to base your interpretation on a number of factors called deception cues. Knowing these cues can help you in two important ways. They will help you spot a liar, and they will help you learn the body language cues to establish credibility.

Nonverbal Deception Cues

The Nine Months Pregnant Pause — Pauses

Liars use longer pauses, shorter answers and longer times between a question and a response than someone who is merely nervous. It makes sense that liars need time to create the lie; recalling the truth takes less time. If you ask a clerk if he gave you the correct change and there is a long pause before his response, it may be an indication of deceit. However, this is not a cue you should take in isolation. You might also check to see where his eyes go after you ask the question. People tend to look up to the right to visualize or create a new response or down to the right to create the sounds of a new response. We recall information that occurred in the past by looking up to the left or down to the left. Spot a liar by listening for pauses and right eye movement. Be credible by answering spontaneously.

The Hands Have it — Excessive Gesturing and Adaptors

When people lie spontaneously, they tend to spend more time gesturing with hands and using adapters, such as scratching the body or playing with a pen than someone who is just nervous. If you ask Sara in payroll, why your check is so late, and then she picks up the beanie baby from her desk and begins to play with it as she says she has worked on this for hours and she has no idea, she may be subconsciously saying something else. On the other hand, the rehearsed or practiced liar, who has planned their deceit ahead of time, will try to control gestures. Spot a liar by their excessive gesturing. Be credible by not fidgeting and keeping your gestures natural.

Mind Your Mouth — Mouth, Lips, and Tongue Cues

Be careful of pursing or licking your lips. Congressman Gary Condit pursed his lips and sucked them inward more than 14 times in his infamous 2002 television interview with Connie Chung. This behavior can indicate extreme anxiety as well as withholding information and may also be a sign of aggression. Tight lips indicate you may be planning to hold the truth in. If you actually suck the lips part way in, you may be withholding anger. When you are nervous, your mouth becomes dry, and you lick your lips and swallow as you struggle to find the right words to say. To spot a liar, look for unusual movement of the mouth, lips or tongue. To be credible, don't lick or purse your lips and keep yourself hydrated with plenty of water.

Be Still, My Love — Lack of Animation

Deception is all about keeping something hidden. The more a person moves his body or expresses with his voice and the more he or she speaks, the more we can learn. Practiced liars know this and usually keep as still as possible. Being overly controlled can work against you. Gary Condit was coached to stay still in his television interview, so he kept his face inexpressive, his upper body stiff, and his legs crossed. First, he looked frozen, and then when he couldn't hold it any longer, he leaked out aggression cues such as finger pointing, grasping motions, and sticking out his tongue. We spotted a liar. I have often seen a normally animated customer service rep begin to do a product explanation and become a monotonous automaton. The audience wondered what he was hiding and was bored to tears. Spot a liar by looking for someone who is too stiff and still. Be credible by making sure you are animated.

Hand Jive — Hiding Hands

The hands come out symbolically from the heart; hands and arms symbolically express the emotions of the heart. Liars tend to keep their hands hidden and still. They stick them in their pockets, clench them together or hold them behind their backs. Imagine that the person whom you suspect of lying has the truth in the palms of his hands and see if he shows them to you. It is not surprising that one of the first things we do to start a business interaction or close a deal with a customer is shake hands. My three years of research on handshakes shows that the single most important factor in the handshake is palm to palm contact. Research also indicates that if customers don't get this contact, they wonder what the other person is hiding, they are uncomfortable for the rest of the interaction, and they are less likely to purchase. People often do hide their hands when they are nervous, so if you see hidden hands, ask yourself why that person is nervous. Be credible by using your hands normally as you speak or by letting them hang loosely at your sides. And try not to clasp them together. Body language is highly symbolic, and clasping may look as if you are holding your own hands for comfort.

Windows to the Soul — Closed Curtains

We have what I call windows all over the body. Just as we pull down the shades when we don't want others to see in, we also close off the entrances to our bodies so our true feelings aren't revealed. There are windows at the bottom of the feet, the kneecaps, the bottom of the torso, the middle of the chest, the neck, the mouth and eyes, and the top of the head. Liars tend to close entrances to hide the truth. A liar closes these windows by putting clothing over them, turning his body away from the person he is talking to, putting objects or furniture between himself and others and, most simply, by folding his arms. When someone's windows are closed, we don't feel as comfortable in an interaction. If someone has her face turned toward you, but the rest of her body is turned toward the exit, her windows are closed. She is saying, "I am pretending by looking at you that I want to talk but actually I want to go home. I am not really interested in serving you."

In the 90's I consulted with the architect and owners of the new "Ripley's Believe It or Not" museums on the layout of the entrances and ticket counters of new locations. They planned to make raised, platform-high, counter-top ticket booths an average of ten steps from the door. This design was great for security, but I explained that this design would reduce spontaneous purchases. People had to go too far to see the ticket person, and most of his or her body windows would be hidden. Customers would not feel safe and comfortable. To spot a liar, look for barriers and closed windows. To be credible, keep your windows open.

Why Can't We Be Friends? — Withdrawn Behavior

If we are comfortable with ourselves, the person we are with, and the topic we are discussing, we will be open and friendly. Liars don't usually feel very comfortable so they tend to hold back and be less friendly. It is easier for friends and intimates to lie to each other successfully because they appear less withdrawn and friendlier. Perhaps they concentrate more on lying because the other person knows them, perhaps they are more concerned about the consequences of detection or maybe they are better at deception because they have experience lying to the person in the past. In any case, they lie differently, and as with career criminals, they can usually maintain a more relaxed overall demeanor and look the recipient of the lie straight in the eye. Strangers need to work harder to keep each other from seeing the truth. Consequently, they are more withdrawn and closed off from the person with whom they are conversing and usually don't appear as friendly. You have heard for years that you need to be friendly with the customer. Now you know why. Remember, our ancestors went to the friendly tribes to trade. To spot a liar, look for someone unfriendly. Be credible by reaching out, being open and receptive.

I Want To Sell You A Car! — Excessive Confidence

Have you ever encountered a super-smooth salesperson? Perhaps, he or she over- enthusiastically praised the product, and you felt uncomfortable about the pitch. Then you have deciphered a lie by noting that the person sounded too good or too confident. We look and listen for anything that doesn't sound normal. Nonverbal communication, in this case *paralanguage*, which includes voice, tone, volume, and speaking rate, that sounds overconfident or "staged" is read at the subconscious level as out of the norm. Years ago, a friend who was a very successful computer salesman came to my office to do some selling for me over the phone. Instead of using a planned patter, he hemmed and hawed and stumbled over his words. His mistakes surprised me. I thought he was just warming up. Five calls later he was still sounding awkward. So I gathered up my courage and asked him about his behavior. He said, "Oh, when I first started as a salesman I was very awkward and very successful. People went out of their way to be nice to me on the phone. Sometimes they even finished my sales pitch for me! I noticed later when I became very confident, make that cocky and fake, that I was not as successful. So I stayed humble. I don't worry about sounding smooth and perfect. Just being my bumbling self works for me." Spot a liar by going with your gut impression. Your instincts can read fake at a hundred paces. Normal levels of confidence, however, also read as sincere. Be credible by being your real self.

Don't Cry For Me, Argentina — Circumstances Not Matching Demeanor

One of the first things you look for when reading body language is the alignment of the circumstances with the demeanor of the person talking to you. For instance, in Connie Chung's television interview with Congressman Gary Condit, we expected him to be emotionally upset and embarrassed, considering he was a politician suspected of having an affair with a young woman who had been missing for 115 days. Instead, he began the interview calmly and proceeded to become indignant. This demeanor was not what we expected. Lack of appropriateness is a sign that the person is not being sincere. When I was driving back from New York a few days after September 11, gas station attendants continued to say with feigned brightness, "Have a nice day." They were on automatic pilot. I knew they didn't even realize how they sounded. Oddly enough when I told them that I was coming back from New York near Ground Zero, each and every person became more sincere. Spot a liar or more accurately spot an insincere person by their use of "canned" or stock phrases. Be credible by treating each person as an individual and being in the moment with them.

Nothing Is Wrong! —
Nonverbal Behavior Does Not Match Spoken Words

When the spoken words don't agree with the nonverbal communication, we generally trust the nonverbal communication to tell us the truth. When a customer says nothing is wrong, while sitting with arms wrapped tightly around the body and a scowl on the face, we doubt her sincerity. If a service rep says, "Yes, we can do that for you" while shaking his head "No," we can be sure he is, at least, ambivalent about his answer. Spot a liar by watching for lack of synchronicity. The subconscious reveals the truth. If the service person says, "This is a great service contract," while rubbing his eyes, it doesn't look right; the ears, it doesn't sound right; or the nose, it stinks. Look credible by matching your body language to what you are saying.

These days getting a front-line service representative to love their jobs and enjoy dealing with the customers can be difficult. Attitude problems and surly help seem be the norm. You can't just tell the help to smile. Employees need to be comfortable with their tasks and knowledge. Ask yourself, "Am I giving enough time to training and what am

I doing to make the workplace friendly?"

A smile is the most common facial expression for masking emotions. It is often used to hide displeasure and anger. A genuine smile changes the entire face. The eyes light up. The forehead wrinkles, the eyebrows and cheek muscles rise, skin around the eyes and mouth crinkles and finally the mouth turns up. In a masking smile, however, nothing moves but the corners of the mouth and often they curve down rather than up. When you or your employees are happy working with people and believe in what you are saying and selling, your smile will be genuine, and customers will be more likely to return that smile.

Knowing these cues can help you decipher when someone else is being less than honest. Sometimes people say, "It's all in your mind." Now you know, "It's all in your body."

Answers:

Answer c. Liars have longer pauses, shorter answers and longer times between a question and a response than someone who is merely nervous.

Answer b. Our faces and eyes hide the truth more easily than the rest of the body. The body, especially the lower portion, is under less conscious control.

Answer c. Your body language needs to match what you're saying.

Answer c. Keep your palms open. Rehearsed liars tend to keep their hands, especially the palms, hidden and still. Loosely at your sides is all right.

Answer a. Leaning toward the interviewer makes you appear open and interested. Liars tend to close entrances to the body to hide the truth.

Answer c. Be careful of pursing or licking your lips. A smile is the most common facial expression used to mask emotions.

ABOUT PATTI WOOD, CSP

*P*atti Wood, M.A.,CSP is an international speaker and trainer. Since 1982 she has designed and conducted keynote speeches, workshops and convention seminars for hundreds of top companies and national associations including AT&T, GTE, Chick-fil-A, Merk Pharmaceuticals, Dupont, Lucent Technologies, and Kroger. She delivers more than 100 presentations a year. Clients describe her as a dynamic, high-energy, powerhouse presenter. Patti develops information-packed, high-energy, laughter-filled relationships with participants that leaves them talking in the halls about what they have learned. Patti has been researching, writing and speaking on nonverbal communication for more than 20 years. She taught communication at the university level for 11 years. She is interviewed frequently by the media, including CBS and ABC radio news, the BBC, PBS, Entrepreneur *magazine*, Woman's World, Cosmopolitan, The National Examiner, YM, *and* Expert *magazine as a body language expert.* Time *magazine recognized her nonverbal communication course at Florida State University as one of the top college courses in the country. She is a communication consultant for* US Weekly *and she has authored or co-authored 11 books.*

Contact Information:
Patti Wood
2312 Hunting Valley Drive
Decatur, GA 30033
Phone: (404) 371-8228
E-mail: Pattiwood@PattiWood.com
Website: www.PattiWood.com
                www.TheBodyLanguageLady.com

WHO'S RIGHT?
A Radical Approach to Satisfying Your Most Difficult Customers

by Michael Connor

An Insight

"**W**hat if there's nobody out there?" The statement slipped past my usually reliable defenses and almost knocked me off my seat. Breezed right in and blew apart some of my most basic life-long assumptions regarding myself and how I relate to others. My world would never be quite the same.

I was attending a seminar in St. Petersburg, Russia, of all places. It was September, 1993. Two days later, I found myself watching the Russian Paramount Building (the Russian "White House") burning as a result of political turmoil and economic unrest. It was as if my own inner shift of awareness was being mirrored in the world. Uncertainty lie ahead. I was both excited and fearful regarding the possibilities. I sensed my new realization was a doorway to something extraordinary, an internal revolution.

> *"When we see men of a contrary character,*
> *we should turn inwards and examine ourselves"*
> — Confucius

The Tough Ones

Who are your toughest, most difficult internal and external customers? I'm not talking about the ones who drive a hard bargain. I'm not talking about the ones who are annoying. I'm not even talking about the ones who want it all for nothing. I'm talking about the ones who are unrealistic, never satisfied, don't listen to logic, can't be soothed over with kindness and courtesy, and just don't seem to be living in the same world as you. The ones you just wish would go away — satisfied or not. You know the ones I'm talking about, your stomach churns when they come to mind.

It's important that we're clear about the type of customer I'm referring to here. What I'm about to suggest as an approach is, well, radical. It's not that it won't work with other customers. In fact, it may well be the norm in all important business relationships in ten years. However, it takes not only highly committed and (dare I say?) highly evolved customer service managers and representatives, but also a willingness to look way outside the box. Outside the box far enough to consider the question, "What if there's nobody out there?".

> *"You're not in the world, the world is in you."*
>
> — Deepak Chopra

A Radical Notion

It's not uncommon, over time, for the esoteric to travel from the depths of absurdity and science fiction into the realms of "cutting edge" technology and on into mainstream thinking. You can see it everywhere around you. It is also true that relatively few investors, CEO's, and Board of Directors are willing to invest time and money into notions that are counter to much, if not all, of their conventional thinking and experience. Columbus's ability to secure financing and governmental support remains one of history's greatest demonstrations of entrepreneurial vision and salesmanship. Remember — the world *was* flat in the minds of people back then.

"What if there's nobody out there?" means that when we look out into the world, the only thing we really see is ourselves. The universe is one big mirror. The people, the places, the events — all mirroring something inside of us. Sometimes the mirror is literal, although most of the time it is metaphoric.

I might find myself judging someone who is overweight, for example, and, at least initially, may not see how it mirrors anything about me because I am physically fit. If I am willing to be more honest and look more deeply, however, I might begin to see that the judgment is not so much about the weight but about the lack of control or addictive pattern that is the cause of the weight. With this awareness I can begin to see some of the areas in my own life where I lack discipline and, more importantly, the negative judgment I hold. My new awareness not only allows me to take ownership of the judgment, but also empowers me by placing the issue in the only place I can actually do something about it — within me.

I know for some it's a big leap, and this is where many are tempted to stop listening or stop reading because this concept is either too confronting or too weird. If you're one of those tempted to stop here, let me assure you, it *is* both confronting and *can* appear weird, and I invite you to continue reading. I invite you to continue reading because if you are willing to implement this approach, you may find it beginning to revolutionize the communications throughout your organization. You may find yourself ten years ahead of your competitors in terms of problem-solving, team-building, and overall productivity. You might even have that knot in your stomach go away.

> *"I bid him look into the lives of men as though into a mirror,*
> *and from others to take an example of himself."*
> — Terence, 190-159 B.C.

Accountability

Nearly every successful organization I've worked with encourages accountability. Some profess the virtues of total accountability. But very few, if any, take accountability to the level that suggests that each one of us is totally accountable for everything that happens to us. An approach that suggests that everyone we come in contact with, every situation we encounter, every outcome we experience we have, somehow, created.

The reason few of us are willing to venture into the land of true accountability is that it is both confronting, and, at least initially, illogical. How, in a world filled with so many uncontrollable factors, can I possibly be responsible for it all? In the paradigm within which most of us live, most of the time, total accountability doesn't make sense. We've been conditioned to see ourselves as victims, as small people in a big universe beyond our control. Most of us prefer it that way. Victims get sympathy. Accountable people get blamed. It's easier to make it about someone or something else. It's easier because if it's about someone or something else, then I don't need to change anything about myself. I get to stay safe and I get to be "right."

Unfortunately, being "right" usually means making someone else "wrong," and while this approach can give us a short-term sense of control, its effect on relationships, both personal and professional, is devastating. When it comes to customer relations, being "right" is paramount to saying goodbye, both to that customer and anyone with whom they associate. No one likes to feel "wrong" — least of all someone who is paying for your services.

The notion of total accountability can only begin to make sense when we realize that the great majority of what occurs in our life we create unconsciously. A lifetime of stored images, conditioning, and beliefs create a filter through which we, primarily unconsciously, draw to us people, circumstances, and events. Ironically, it is only when we begin to acknowledge that we, in fact, are responsible for our lives, that we can begin to see how we create, both consciously and unconsciously, the events and circumstances that, until now, we might have described as either accident or coincidence.

"Mirrors should reflect a little before throwing back images."
— Jean Cocteau

The Totally Accountable Team

You may be asking, by this point, assuming you've made it this far, "All this mirror and total accountability stuff is interesting (or not), but — enough already — tell me how it's going to satisfy my toughest customers." You may find the answer, while simple to communicate in words, to be one of your most challenging and, at the same time, most rewarding undertakings. The key to success will hinge on the people that make up your customer service team and the people to whom they report. There is no such thing as a totally accountable system or method, but there are people who are willing to be totally accountable. You must be one of them, and you must surround yourself with others.

Since most people will profess to the virtues of being accountable, and yet so few truly are, how do you differentiate those who mouth accountability from those fully committed to practicing it? Note that I said "practicing" it. Here's a step-by-step process to guide you in pulling together and developing a highly accountable team:

1. Ask yourself if you are fully committed to being accountable. This is a not a commitment to be taken lightly, and it's one you'll need to recommit to every day. Be honest with yourself.

2. Be accountable not just for your actions and results, but for your feelings and judgments about people and events around you. A negative reaction to someone or something will almost always let you know of a negative judgment you hold inside.

3. As you demonstrate greater honesty, accountability, and ownership, notice what others around you begin to do and what your intuition tells you about people. Not only will you naturally begin to attract to you more accountable people, but you will also have a much better "sense" of people's nature.

4. Seek out people who have a natural desire to want to understand themselves and others more deeply, and who want to assist or be or service to others.

5. Put potential team members into challenging or stressful scenarios, situations, or interactions and observe whether they tend towards accountability or blame.

6. Following the process in #5, ask them what they observed in someone else that is a mirror of something within themselves. Notice who is willing to really take a look, acknowledge their judgments or shortcomings, and communicate from honesty and accountability.

7. Remember that the willingness to be fully accountable is the key. Anyone who claims to be already fully accountable doesn't understand the level of accountability we're referring to here (it can only be practiced, never mastered).

8. Choose your team based both on your observations and intuition. Honesty and accountability can be identified more successfully by your intuitive sense of a person than by the words they say (I refer you again to #3).

9. Create a series of guidelines with your team that reinforce accountability on an ongoing basis (see below). Since team members will be internal customers to one another, a great place to start fully accountable customer service is with one another.

10. Support one another in remembering that true accountability is a process that requires commitment and awareness every day.

It's worth noting that pulling together team members who are willing to be fully accountable and providing the structure (guidelines) and support necessary is 90 percent of the process. Those who yearn for greater self-understanding and who have a desire to assist others will begin to recognize accountability as the foundation for both. They will look forward to the opportunity to work with your toughest customers, and will realize that satisfying these unsatisfiable customers will go hand-in-hand with greater self-awareness. Their approach will have little to do with the approaches that work with most of your customers (since you've tried all these approaches already). Being responsive, giving them what they've asked for, and being courteous haven't done the trick, have they? Your team will know that the only place that a meaningful shift can occur is within themselves, and that when that shift occurs, it will be mirrored by the customer. We'll take a more detailed look at how this happens in a moment, but first let's explore more fully why commitment and support are so essential in making all this work.

While seeing everything as a mirror seems like a simple enough thing to do, the concept of total accountability is extremely confronting to the part of our nature that doesn't want to change. This part of us wants to do things the way we've always done them, not only because it's easier, but also because we somehow believe it's safer. The logic of our survival-driven "reptillian" brain is simple: if I've done it before and I'm alive, it must be ok; if I haven't done it before, there's a risk. Uncertainty is associated with death at this basic level of consciousness. Its job is to keep us safe, and it (the survival-based aspect) will do everything it can to move us back into conditioned patterns and habits that it has deemed safe. The challenge is to stay conscious in the face of a very strong inner force that pulls us back into old, unconscious thinking and behaviors.

An effective set of guidelines serves the purpose of keeping you and your team conscious and aware regarding accountability and the mirror of life. Developing, along with your team, your own set of guidelines is suggested, both to tailor the structure to your own unique needs as well as to establish ownership in the guidelines themselves. Below is a sample set that you might use as a starting point with your team:

1. Be willing to be accountable for it all (see it all as a mirror).

2. Become aware of and own your judgments and feelings.

3. Build trust by keeping your word.

4. Communicate openly and honestly, remembering there is no true honesty without accountability.

5. Assume that everything that shows up is there to assist you in learning and growing.

6. Constantly practice acceptance of self and others.

7. Remember it's not about solving a problem, it's about bringing awareness and understanding (judgment can't be solved through more judgment).

8. Maintain the awareness that the only true change happens internally.

9. Remind yourself and others that it's a process, a practice.

10. Your primary intention is to accept and love it all.

"Out beyond right and wrong there is a field. I'll meet you there."

— Rumi

From Judgment to Acceptance to Love: The Critical Shift

Your toughest customers, just like the toughest people in all areas of your life, tend to experience a great deal of judgment. Certainly you are not the only one who finds them difficult to deal with. Criticism and judgment have a way of interlocking themselves in an interesting and unique fashion. When we attempt to stop judging, we usually find ourselves judging the judgment we already hold, exacerbating it. Judgment and criticism are especially tricky because they often hide behind denial. Somewhere, sometime, we experienced stinging, painful criticism and believed it. That belief about ourselves, that self-image, was too painful to deal with, so we pushed it down, out of our awareness. Hidden, but not gone. Unconsciously, we'll draw to us people and situations that mirror that judgment. We'll be reminded of our hurt, and attack, putting that same judgment out on the person or event that mirrored it. It's simply too painful to take ownership of, although the great majority of people aren't thinking in terms of ownership and accountability to begin with.

The job of your team is never to attempt to change anything about the difficult customer. Every attempt to change their behavior has failed, and for good reason. Most attempts to change someone else are motivated by judgment, and usually fails miserably, resulting in more judgment. Their job is to fully accept the person exactly as they are. Acceptance doesn't mean resignation or tolerance. It means fully accepting, which, while easy to do if you have no judgment of your own, can be quite challenging if you're like most human beings. Here are the steps that will assist you and your team, making this essential shift:

1. Prior to contact with the customer, recommit to accountability and seeing it all as a mirror.

2. Ask, listen to, and observe the customer with an intent to understand, not solve.* Utilize reflective listening techniques to clarify, when necessary.

3. Observe and make note of your own inner reactions, feelings, and judgments with an intent to understand, not solve.

4. If necessary, share your reactions, feelings, and judgments with a team member to gain greater clarity and ownership.

5. Accept your feelings and judgments as part of being human, allowing for compassion and forgiveness when necessary. Get support when needed.

6. Since there is no place for judgment to live in the realm of unconditional acceptance, the judgments and negative feelings will fade and will begin to be replaced by love.

7. Your self-acceptance and self-love will be mirrored out into your universe, including your toughest customers.

8. Your own self-acceptance and self-love will allow you to accept and love them exactly as they are, giving them the same gift you gave yourself.

*Clearly, if there is a specific or technical request for a product or service, you'll handle that if possible. I'm referring to our tendency to want to "fix" the person whose behavior is annoying.

9. Their judgments and negative behavior will shift because there will be no place for them to live in the realm of unconditional acceptance and love.

10. Start again — remembering it's a process.

The beauty of any mirror is that it will change its reflection when we change. When we shift from self-righteousness and judgment into acceptance and self-love, our life will reflect that — including the most difficult people we deal with. Your toughest customers aren't looking for solutions, they're looking for acceptance and love. While they'll never tell you that because they're not aware of it themselves, you'll have a tough time satisfying them with anything else. Your more easily satisfied customers are no different, they are just able to receive it more easily. Since they are reasonable, understanding, and more accepting people to begin with, their world mirrors that back.

"Your vision will become clear only when you can look into your own heart. Who looks outside, dreams; who looks inside, awakes."

— Carl Jung

Self-Love as a Business Principle?

I know that many will find this approach too heart-centered, too strange, and/or too "soft." "Hey Mike, I'm running a business here, not a psychotherapy practice," I can hear some of you saying. So here's my suggestion regarding everything I've shared: *Don't believe me.* Keep doing what you've been doing, if it works. But if you continue to struggle with difficult customers — be they internal (co-workers, managers, project leaders, etc.) or external (retail or business-to-business), then I have one other suggestion: *Don't disbelieve me either. Check it out for yourself.*

You might just start a business revolution.

ABOUT MICHAEL CONNOR

*M*ichael Connor is the president of Creative Transitions: Transforming *Challenges into Opportunities, a company specializing in assisting organizations, teams, and individuals in thriving, excelling, and profiting in the midst of change. He has designed and presented keynotes and training programs around the world since 1993. Mike is the former President and CEO of the Insight Educational Institute and a lead facilitator for Insight Seminars Worldwide. A former health care executive with a wealth of business and management expertise, Mike has presented on four continents. He holds Masters Degrees in Health Care Management and Practical Theology. While consulting to the Ministry of Health in Bulgaria, he met his wife, Maria, a physician. With their two children, they live near Boston.*

Contact Information:
Michael Connor
Creative Transitions
8 Nauset Road
Brockton, MA 02301
Phone: (508) 584-9062
Fax: (508) 580-6466
E-mail: MC@ThriveOnChange.com
Website: www.ThriveOnChange.com

STRESS RELIEF STRATEGIES IN CUSTOMER SERVICE

by Steve Coscia

During my 20 years of managing customer service, I have handled just about every service situation imaginable. These include handling upset customers, and sometimes their lawyers, or federal and state attorneys general. These litigious situations were difficult and very stressful, yet I maintained my professional demeanor throughout. The most difficult situations taught me an important lesson — each stressful experience that we overcome prepares us to handle the stress experiences that lie ahead.

The manifestations of stress in customer service are similar, regardless of your industry or demographics. When stressed, people communicate poorly, become impatient, arrive late, take too many sick days, and often leave early, to say nothing about becoming jumpy, easily irritated, discouraged, or even depressed. These reactions to stress create problems because the role of a customer service person is to assist, satisfy, and convey something positive about themselves and the companies that they represent.

The ideas in this chapter focus on the human side of stress relief. My extensive customer service experience has taught me a simple guiding principle: We invite the type of behavior that we convey towards others. This means that using a wrong word or conveying a bad attitude or an inappropriate tone of voice often invites bad behavior from customers. Therefore, the best proactive strategy for stress relief is to avoid creating stress in the first place. So minimizing stress in customer service begins with recognizing our own conduct and understanding our power to either contain or exacerbate these events. This thought process is very difficult since rational thinking is often the first thing to go when we get stressed.

Fight or Flight

I conducted a survey on stress in the customer service industry. I wanted to bring to the surface the physical and emotional manifestations of stress in the customer service environment, so I asked front-line people. Almost half (47%) of the responses indicated the number one cause of stress in their jobs was calls from irate or difficult customers. That makes sense because that type of behavior triggers our fight-or-flight response. Our fight-or-flight mechanism is our stress response to dangerous events. When we feel threatened, we either want to fight with or run from whatever might be causing us the harm. Our body facilitates this action through the release of hormones that speed up our metabolism and prepare us for battle or a speedy retreat. The challenging part of this fight-or-flight response is that our body doesn't do a good job of distinguishing the difference between real danger, such as when we are being chased by a wild animal, or perceived danger, such as when we handle an angry caller. Over the telephone, when we have the perception that the other person is angry or annoyed and is taking it out on us, this instigates our fight-or-flight response. In a customer service environment you can't run away or fight with a customer, but the body creates psychological manifestations of these reactions. We go through psychological fight-or-flight. Psychological fight might include being snippy over the telephone, arguing with the other person, or trying to "get even" in small ways. These reactions annoy the other person and make his or her behavior even worse. Being retaliatory and snippy over the telephone only gives the other person justification to become even angrier. Now the person can say, "Everything I thought about you and your company is true based on what I'm hearing." This condition only gets us into more trouble and increases our stress level.

Psychological flight often manifests itself as apathy. We run away from the situation. We say to ourselves, "I'm out of here. This is your problem." We stop getting involved. We stop listening. We shut down on trying to be empathetic and no longer try to understand the other person's motivation, intent, and feelings. Listening skills are paramount in enabling us to understand the other person and to determine what we can do to resolve the problem.

Make Time to Think

As professionals we are very big on doing. We love to get things done. I have been saying for years that thinking is highly underrated. I don't think people invest enough time sitting in a quiet place, being alone, and just thinking. So I urge you throughout this chapter to take some of my ideas, write them down, and find time to be alone and think about them. You will be rewarded for the investment you make in some quiet time to think.

React or Respond

Thinking rationally about stress includes believing that you have choices. In customer service, when customers get upset, you have two choices. You can react to what a person has done or you can respond. Anyone can react to an adverse event by simply doing what feels natural. If someone yells at you, you start yelling back. A reaction like this doesn't take much work or thinking on your part. In addition, a reaction is your retaliation for the customer's bad behavior. One of the biggest mistakes we can make is believing that the customer's behavior is the problem. The customer's behavior is NOT the problem. The problem is whatever is causing the customer to behave that way and that's what we should focus on. So fixing the real problem will inevitably fix the customer's behavior. If we choose to react, our voice gets louder, we'll speak faster, we'll become defensive, and we will retaliate. These reactions are inappropriate and unprofessional.

However, a response to an adverse event takes a little more effort.

If we choose to respond, then we'll have to think rationally about what is happening, consider our best options, and then execute a plan. This process includes forcing ourselves to breathe slowly and speak slowly, which gives us more time to select the correct words and stay within the parameters of the guiding principle. If we choose to respond, we'll let the customer vent, listen actively, and manage our tone.

Attitude and Aptitude

In the course of a usual workday in customer service, you go through a productivity curve. As our body works its way into the rhythm of a day, our productivity curve, under usual conditions, increases throughout the day. However, when people get stressed, the productivity curve starts to level off. When this happens, we begin operating at a diminished level of efficiency. We all do this at varying degrees because we all respond to stressful situations differently. One person's mild inconvenience is the other person's major catastrophe.

There are two primary factors that drive our productivity. They are our attitude and our aptitude. Unfortunately, both our attitude and aptitude are affected right from the start when we get stressed out. Our attitude is affected when the productivity curve starts to level off because we start to lose sensitivity. That's the negative attitude that says, "I don't care." "You're interrupting me." "I don't have time for this." "Why are you calling me?" Keep in mind, these words may never be spoken but the customer can hear the inference in the tone of voice. Over the telephone, you can't see the other person, but the tone conveys most of what the customers hear. Telephone communication is not what you say but what the other person hears and thinks you mean. So 80 percent of what you convey is the tone; about 20 percent is the content or the words. Conveying a helpful tone, no matter how we feel, is a first step for staying within the parameters of our guiding principle. By focusing on conveying something nice, no matter how we feel, we will invite back nicer behavior from the other person and inevitably experience less stress.

The second factor to suffer is aptitude. This is the customer service person's ability to analyze and resolve problems. When the fight-or-flight response kicks in, rational thinking goes out the window. In this state, we become preoccupied with our own survival and how fast we can escape the adversity. The welfare of others becomes secondary. In this irrational condition, a person will do what is expedient, not correct. Unfortunately, the expedient route may not be best for the organization. Without the ability to think rationally, we become ineffective. Our active listening skills suffer along with our ability to ascertain all the facts we need to do our job. We become incapable of resolving the customer's real problem or answering the customer's question.

Anger is Never an Option

In my stress survey, about half the respondents said that calls from irate customers were their number one cause of stress. The manifestation of the stress when dealing with an irate customer is often anger. In customer service, anger is never an option. When we become angry, we will make the best speech we'll ever regret. During a typical workday, you probably speak with scores of customers and most of them are polite. A few might be difficult, but your job is bearable. The difficult ones don't push you too far over the edge; however, each negative phone call that you handle is like an annoying drop of water dripping into a bucket. It's a bother. Nothing you can't handle, but these drops keep collecting in the bucket. One customer yells at you because the product he just received was damaged. Another customer yells because of a repetitive invoicing problem. Drip, drip, drip. Eventually you get enough of these drops of water and they start to fill up your bucket. During one phone call a person uses a mannerism or word that pushes your stress button and SPLASH. The bucket spills over with an uncontrolled stream of angry words and behavior. Anger only fuels the worker's need to retaliate. Customers can hear the anger, so they get more upset and everybody gets even more stressed. This is a cycle that we need to break by never allowing ourselves to become angry in the first place.

I hear customer service representatives say, "The customer made me become angry." or "Look what that customer made me do." The flaw in both of these statements is the obvious omission of personal responsibility. We all make choices about our behavior. No one can make us do anything. When we become angry, it is because we have made a conscious choice to do so. So the best rule about anger in customer service is never get there in the first place. Anger is never an option in customer service.

Proper Diet

I used to think that it had to be the customers who made me so jumpy, irritable, and angry. Then, on a day that I was a little too busy to get away from my desk to get that fourth, fifth, or sixth cup of coffee, I learned that I was a little less jumpy and a little less irritable. I was able to handle those difficult calls without getting as stressed out. I started to think that perhaps my diet was contributing to the amount of stress that I was experiencing. So I became more proactive, and I started to minimize the amount of coffee that I was drinking on the job. As a result, I had an easier time maintaining my own metabolism and my response to adverse events. Then I learned afterwards that caffeine causes the adrenal gland to overproduce and secrete epinephrine — one of the stress hormones. So caffeine is a substance that can trigger our stress response inappropriately. Caffeine also speeds up the nervous system, which results in hyper-alertness and in more susceptibility to perceived stress. Caffeine is found in soft drinks, coffee, tea, and chocolate. Think about what you are consuming in the course of the workday. Also, watch your sugar intake. Sugar may give you a quick energy boost, but the effect soon wears off, leaving you more tired and irritable, anxious, or even depressed. In addition, excessive simple sugars in the body tend to deplete the body's vitamin stores, so find ways to eat more fruits and more vegetables and maintain a more balanced diet. In addition, always eat a good breakfast. Your body needs energy after going for about eight hours without food. Skipping breakfast can make you feel tired and it can cause headaches. Eating a good breakfast will give you energy and keep you alert for the day's challenges. You must first feed the stomach, before you can feed the mind. Follow these three guidelines for healthy eating: (1) Eat a diet low in fat, (2) eat five fruits and vegetables a day and (3) eat a variety of foods.

Physical conditioning is also an important part of handling stress well. Being physically active is one of the proactive things I do to maintain a balance in my work and personal life. Structural engineers have learned that pre-stressing materials, such as high beams, steel corrugated flooring, and steel cabling before the assembly of buildings or bridges, is beneficial. Pre-stressing material by applying the loads that will come when the structure is completed will enable that structure to better withstand pressure when it is completed and in use. Good physical conditioning can accomplish the same thing. A person who is in good physical condition will withstand the physical changes that arise during stressful events.

Self Talk

Customer service professionals talk to themselves often. This is called "self-talk." Customer service people have a nasty habit of engaging in very negative and condescending self-talk. Sure, we all make mistakes, but this doesn't mean that we have to beat ourselves over the head each time something goes wrong. Customer service professionals need to learn to change the negative self-talk to positive. Most customer service people will replay the bad experiences and mishandled events in their heads over and over again. Doing this causes them to relive that negative outcome, not just once but numerous times. This is irrational thinking, and this habit will have a cumulative and negative effect on performance and on personal behavior.

I have developed a strategy of overcoming my negative self-talk by forcing myself to smile whenever I find myself engaged in negative self-talk. I have learned that forcing myself to smile does two things. The smile is a reflection of my feelings, but the smile also changes the way I feel. The facial muscles will affect my attitude. So by forcing myself to smile and by changing the self-talk from negative to positive, I start to change my attitude and how I feel. This is a habit that I have developed while I'm driving my car or when I'm alone. This has worked for me in changing my negative attitudes to positive attitudes. It's a habit, and most habits take about 21 days to develop. If you start developing this habit right away today, you will achieve positive results just as I have.

Honesty and Integrity

Maintaining a high level of honesty and integrity in customer service is another way to be proactive and to minimize stress. It is better to disappoint a customer with the truth than to satisfy a customer with a lie. We have all been in those situations where it was easier to just fudge the facts, and tell customers what we thought they wanted to hear. But I have learned it's better to disappoint them. Customers will appreciate knowing what the situation really is, and being honest is the only way to develop real trust between your company and your customers. A customer service professional should do nothing that requires a lie about later on because lying creates more and more stress. Maintaining a high level of honesty and integrity, no matter what, seems like a challenging and difficult choice, but it's one of the proactive things we can do to develop great relationships and minimize some of the stress level.

Keep a Tidy Workspace

Being neat, structured, and orderly is another way to minimize stress. Look around your desk or your cubicle. Are there piles of papers, coffee stains, and Post-It notes? Are things chaotic? I have found that chaos adds to stress. A practice that works for me is to reserve five to ten minutes at the end of my work day to reorganize my desk, to put things into neat piles, to throw away things I don't really need, and to file pieces of paper away. The next morning when I come in I can start the day fresh. Throughout the day, try to find one or two-minute blocks of time when I can organize, throw things away, and file away pieces of paper. This practice becomes a habit and it helps to minimize the level of stress I experience in customer service.

Conclusion

It is easiest to get the job done when we stay within the parameters of my principle that we invite the type of behavior that we convey towards others. Minimizing stress in customer service starts with conveying a positive attitude so that we will invite back the type of behavior that will minimize our stress and enable us to get the job done. Add this principle to rational and proactive behavior about our choices, our thinking, diet, integrity, and tidiness, and we have a winning strategy for stress relief.

ABOUT STEVE COSCIA

Steve Coscia, president of Coscia Communications, is a 20-year customer service practitioner and telephone skills specialist. He is the author of two popular books, Customer Service Over the Phone *and* TELE-Stress. *Some of the companies that use his telephone strategies are Motorola, Milwaukee Power Tools and Olive Garden Restaurants. An avid researcher of customer service trends, Steve conducted one of the industry's first studies of stress in the customer service environment. This survey revealed the causes of stress and many common manifestations of post-stress behavior among customer service professionals. A member of the National Speaker's Association, Steve conducts educational sessions and seminars at conferences and universities worldwide. In addition, he presents keynote speeches, conducts training seminars, and leads telephone skills workshops.*

Contact Information:
Steve Coscia
Coscia Communications Inc.
1605 Melrose Avenue
Havertown, PA 19083
Phone: (610) 853-9836
Fax: (610) 853-1657
E-mail: steve@coscia.com
Website: www.coscia.com

CASH IN
ON CUSTOMER SERVICE

by Paul Johnson

When your company delivers good customer service, you deserve to win more new business. Most companies overlook this great revenue opportunity that their customer service efforts can create for them. What's really a shame is that they're wasting an opportunity they've *already paid for* through their investments in customer service.

Our customers may be happy, satisfied, and even loyal, but our products still aren't going to sell themselves. We can focus as much energy and resources as we want on keeping customers happy, and it still costs just as much to sell a new customer.

If you want your company to earn new customers and grow, you need a good offense. Customer service is really a defensive strategy. It helps protect your customer base, engendering loyalty so that your customers are still your customers when they're ready to buy again. Yet most companies don't bother to leverage the investment they make in these customer service programs and projects to make it easier to win new business.

Marilynn Mobley is a speaker, author, and public relations expert, as well as the Head Nut at Acorn Consulting Group. Marilynn is so good at leveraging her current customers to get new customers that she has done little in the way of traditional marketing. In fact, she sells her speaking programs without the benefit of a demo video, an unusual feat in the speaking profession.

If you visit her website at TheAcornGroup.com, you'll find it littered with comments from clients. Marilynn knows that those positive comments bring her business. "More than one prospect has visited my website, called, and said, 'It was the testimonials that led me to call you.'" Marilynn serves her clients well, communicates their rave reviews to prospects, and leverages that into new clients, all without using the expected video.

Maybe someday Marilynn will have a video to make her selling job even easier. But for Marilynn, delivering great customer service and harvesting testimonials have proven to be effective business-building strategies. Brochures, videos, and other promotional materials can come later.

It's time your selling organization started using old customers to make new sales.

Get Offensive with Customer Service

Looking at customer service as the road to revenue may be a new concept to many in your organization, but it's important for several reasons. First of all, salespeople and their managers are always looking for ways to sell more, sell faster, and sell easier. Leveraging customer service can accomplish all three.

If you're an executive looking for new ways to grow year-over-year revenue to satisfy your stockholders, leveraging customer service to promote new sales is an untapped revenue opportunity in almost every company.

Customer service managers who are championing new customer service initiatives may be pleased to find that using customer service to assist your company's selling efforts can provide a rapid return on investment and make it easier to gain approval for those new customer service projects.

We all know that, even with great customer service, you're going to have customer attrition. Revenues will decline unless you pursue sales and marketing to support revenue growth. You have to proactively go out and get business; the only question is, "How?" By hitching your customer service to your selling efforts, you can link that investment right to the top line. Your selling team will welcome the partnership because leveraging customer service makes selling easy.

Here are some of the benefits you'll gain when you cash in on customer service:

- Shorter sales cycles
- Better market penetration
- Faster growth than your competitors as you take market share from them
- Selling success no longer dependent on feature/function shootouts
- Easier-to-get new sales appointments
- Better penetration of accounts as you sell more products and services to each account
- Increased loyalty of current customers for even lower attrition rates
- Improved profit per customer
- Fewer deals stuck in the pipeline
- Competitors too risky for your prospects to consider
- Improved credibility in the marketplace
- Methodical removal of major selling obstacles

When you cash in on customer service, you'll have a less expensive way to sell new customers. You'll gain more new customers, increase your market share, and enjoy substantial revenue growth.

In 1980, When the World Was Flat . . .

In the "olden days," we had local markets, with local customers and local competitors. We had less clutter, less confusion in the marketplace. Because customers had fewer choices, they were willing to forge tighter links with the providers that serviced them. And companies had to provide good customer service because the pace was slower, and there was more time for purchasers to perform due diligence before signing a contract. In the local markets, bad companies had no place to hide. Sometimes we had to put up with shoddy service from "the only game in town," but at least we knew it was bad going in.

Today, globalization offers us more choices. After a while, everything begins to sound the same. As sellers, we can win business both inside and outside our local market, but now our customers are not dense enough, not close enough together, to network by chance. We can't depend on "word of mouth" — our customers talking us up to our prospects — because they don't know each other.

Still, buyers don't want to make decisions based solely on a specification sheet and a salesperson's assurances. They want to hear from somebody besides the seller that the product really works and that the company providing it delivers on promises.

Linda McCulloch is president of Design That Works Communications Inc., a full-service graphic design and advertising agency in Atlanta, Georgia. When working with prospective clients, she makes a point of showing samples of previous work done for other clients. Then, she provides letters from those same clients so that the prospect knows that the clients are happy and got what they paid for.

"One prospect was looking for us to develop an identity package for his company," Linda reports. "I met with him and showed him work we had done for several clients, and then later mailed him letters we received from those same clients. When he called to tell us he was giving us the project, he said, 'The letters in combination with the quality of your work sold us.'"

One Arm Is Tied Behind Your Back

Companies are not leveraging their happy customers to create more new customers because customer service is an operations function and is not linked to sales. Customer service people aren't expected to sell, they're not trained to sell, and we wouldn't expect them to even think about selling as they respond to the issues presented to them all day long.

Leveraging customer service into more new sales is an undertaking that any organization can pursue. While it's not complicated, it can't be left to the individual salespeople to deal with at a tactical level. Instead, an enterprise-wide, strategic approach is called for, as all salespeople will access the elements of this program for the benefit of the entire organization. A project champion, preferably someone with revenue responsibility, should carry the ball for developing this program. Once you determine that the customer service you deliver is worthy of being leveraged to win new sales, it's time to move forward with a step-by-step program using proven tools that work, training that shows your team how to use those tools, and the tactics that will let you win new business without alienating your current customers.

This step-by-step approach is based on letting your customers furnish all the proof your prospects need to make a positive decision. Since prospects can't get the proof from their next-door neighbor anymore, you need to show them who the real people are who are already benefiting from their decision to use your product or service.

As preparation for this selling program, you'll need to collect a variety of proof sources from your current customers to be used during your selling process. Proof sources are the specific selling tools that validate the claims you make to prospects, and show that you can deliver on your promises. These include testimonial letters, audio recordings, case studies, and more. You'll work with your customer service team to collect these proof sources and apply them in your selling efforts. Once prospects have evaluated the product and understand what they'll get for the price you are asking, you'll use proof sources from customers to show your prospect that your claims are true and that it's safe for them to proceed with the purchase.

Take One Giant Step Forward

Let's explore in detail one step in the process, so you can start to cash in on customer service today. We'll begin by identifying the six primary objections that your salespeople face from prospective customers, and then methodically identify customers who have stories you can use to neutralize those objections.

Poll your salespeople to learn the common objections that they hear from prospects. They'll be happy to tell you. You'll hear things like, "Your price is too high." "Your company is too big." "Your competitor has Feature X and you don't." Get a representative sampling from your sales force, and you'll be able to identify the most common objections your sales team faces.

Now present this consolidated list of the most common objections back to the very same salespeople who contributed the responses. This time, ask them to identify the most serious objections: those that have no good response, or that are most difficult to overcome. These objections are stopping your sales team dead in their tracks. And they're so common that if they haven't affected every salesperson already, you can be sure they will. Brian Tracy, an accomplished businessman, consultant, and author, taught me a long time ago that six seems to be the magic number for primary objections, and I have found that to be true over the years. So unless you know a better number, we'll focus on using your customers to resolve the six most serious objections that are commonly presented to your selling team.

Next, focus on one of these objections and identify current customers whose experiences will refute the objection. Go to these customers and ask them to provide you with a proof source, such as a testimonial letter, which invalidates the objection. For example, when somebody tells me, "Your price is too high," I have specific letters that I can show them. One states, "You delivered in record time AND under budget." Another letters says, "The project seemed costly at first, but proved to be a real bargain when we saw the results we received." In this way, you'll be proactively harvesting proof from your customers that is pointed directly at the specific obstacles blocking the road to success for your sales force.

Naturally, you'll want to repeat the same process for each of the primary objections that you identified through surveying your sales force. When you're done, they'll have a set of proof sources at the ready, so that when a prospect brings up one of these primary objections, your sales team will have more than fancy words and cute tricks to try to move past them. They'll have powerful, specific, and real-world proof from your current customers who have chosen to vouch for the validity of your claims. Your prospects will know that they can buy from you with confidence because they can expect great results just like current customers already enjoy.

At the beginning of his sales career, Greg Vetter of Atlanta, Georgia, made 50 cold calls *in person* every day. "I learned that the last person a buyer would trust would be a salesperson. I knew I had to come up with a more efficient way to sell or, if not, buy a lot of stock in a shoe company."

Today Greg runs Vetter Productivity, a professional organizational firm specializing in the processes that free people to naturally work at their peak capacity. When Greg is working with a prospective client, he makes sure that the prospect has somebody to believe besides Greg.

"When I first meet with prospective clients, I do a thorough job of qualifying them to find out what their objections are and the results they want to accomplish," reports Greg. "Then, I access my collection of my top 50 testimonial letters from my past client base and select copies of the letters that speak specifically about how we've delivered the same results this prospect is looking for, as well as for letters that speak to the same objections. I underline salient phrases, recopy the phrases in the margins, and give them to the prospect to call."

The third person always does a much better job of selling Greg's services than he does. It's been a long, long time since Greg has had to make 50 cold calls in a day. As of today, he owns no stock in a shoe company.

Stop Wasting Your Customers' Words

You can also enlist your customer service representatives to help you counter known objections. All day long, your customer service folks are having conversations with your customers. Many times a day, your customers are telling your people positive, complimentary things about your product, and are expounding on the benefits of doing business with you. These positive comments go nowhere because the customer service people don't know what to do with them. They are not aware of the potential good these testimonials could do for the company's selling efforts, nor has management put in place the training or the mechanisms to capture this useful information.

At this very moment, one of your customer service people is hearing some critical insight that would help one of your salespeople win over a new customer tomorrow. The solution is to teach your customer service representatives how to listen for those comments that can support the efforts of your selling organization, and then how to capture that information from the customer in the form of a proof source.

Jeff Multz applied his 17 years of Customer Relationship Management (CRM) consulting experience and made selling easier for the team at Firstwave Technologies, Inc. Jeff is the vice president of product sales for Firstwave and has developed an approach to enlist his 1,100 current customers to help his team sell new accounts.

Firstwave maintains quotes and case studies collected from customers on the company intranet. These powerful quotes are accessible by keyword search from within the office on the company sales toolkit. So, the first step is to get prospective customers to come to a Firstwave office. Then Jeff talks with the prospects to identify their peer group and their pain. Peer group refers to people in similar roles and authority within their same industry. Pain describes the particular problem or challenge that needs to be resolved.

"With that information, I can do a keyword search and pull up a couple dozen quotations on the spot," says Jeff. "I can produce actual quotes that demonstrate that we've already relieved this same pain for many other people. And often, these quotes are from people the prospect knows and cares about because they're all peers in the same industry. From here, we can get down to business in a hurry."

Jeff Multz's selling approach makes the global market seem just as warm and friendly as Main Street back home.

Asking your customer service representatives to identify and collect testimonial letters and other proof from customers will be a new experience for them. After they have been fully trained, you may want to consider an incentive program to reward them for their successes. Here are some ideas to aid in your collection of testimonial letters, excerpted from my booklet, "Let Your Customers Sell You: 120 Tips for Getting and Using Testimonial Letters to Win More Business."

- Offer a bounty, perhaps $25, for each letter that an employee brings in.

- Create some minimum specifications for letters to qualify, such as containing certain desired elements.

- Include additional prizes for major contributors who bring in a lot of letters during a fixed period, perhaps three months. A weekend for two at a resort and the recognition that goes with that will motivate some people more than money.

For some additional help, view the article, "Six Key Elements for a Testimonial Letter," at www.panache-yes.com.

Help Them Believe

While there is more that you can do to make cashing in on customer service a success for your organization, the key is to maintain a coordinated effort that will create variety and depth of proof sources. Most organizations rely almost exclusively on references and a two-step process that works like this:

1. Get a hot prospect.

2. Have the prospect call your best customer.

Some companies do collect testimonial letters, but these are often less effective than they could be. The content is often vague on delivery of actual results, containing instead unsubstantiated superlatives like "you guys are great" and "your product is excellent." This kind of content combined with the inconsistent messages often found in these letters does little to alleviate the prospect's concerns and primary objections.

The important thing to remember is that buyers want to believe salespeople; they just don't think they should. They want to say "Yes" and move forward but they're afraid. You can lower their perceived risk so that they can feel comfortable saying "Yes." Using proof sources, you can show them who besides the selling company says that this deal is a winner. Selling gets easier for you because customer proof sources make buying easier for the prospect.

Make a commitment to cash in on customer service today. You've already invested in the customer service initiatives that are generating happy customers. Right now you're paying your sales team to beat their heads against the wall using conventional sales techniques to bring in business. Start redirecting their efforts towards using proof sources from your happy customers as part of their selling regimen. They'll shorten their sales cycle, lower your cost of customer acquisition, and easily win all the business you deserve.

ABOUT PAUL JOHNSON

Paul Johnson delivers Shortcuts to Yes™ programs to help clients like ADP, Nortel Networks, and Akzo Nobel accelerate their revenue growth. Paul has over 20 years of success helping companies, and the people who work for them, to capitalize on their strengths, gain positive decisions, and increase their earnings. He has been developing and implementing the techniques found in his seminars and workshops since 1984. As principal of Panache and Systems, a sales and marketing consulting firm, Paul has developed a four-part approach that aligns marketing and selling organizations and allows better leverage of all assets, including customer service teams, to bring in more business. He is an expert at getting buyers to say "Yes" during the selling experience by applying proof sources such as testimonial letters. He is author of Let Your Customer Sell You, *a guide to using testimonial letters to win more business.*

Contact Information:
Paul Johnson
Panache and Systems
149 Azalea Chase Drive
Suwanee, GA 30024
Phone: (770) 271-7719
Fax: (770) 271-7493
E-mail: paul.j@panache-yes.com
Website: www.panache-yes.com

WHAT IT TAKES TO GIVE "AND THEN SOME" SERVICE

by Carol A. Kivler

One afternoon while browsing through a card store, I came across a verse that not only changed the way I viewed service but also changed the way I viewed life. The verse is by Carl Holmes and is entitled, "And Then Some." The simplistic words used in the poem send out a strong and valuable message. We don't need to be miles ahead of others to be recognized as superior at what we do; we only need to give, *and then some,* which sometimes is just a half-inch more.

And Then Some

These three little words are the secret to success.
They are the difference between average people
and top people in most companies.
The top people always do what is expected . . .
and then some . . .

They are thoughtful of others, they are considerate and kind . . .
and then some . . .

They meet their obligations and responsibilities fairly and squarely . . .
and then some . . .
they are good friends and helpful neighbors . . .
and then some.
They can be counted on in an emergency . . .
and then some . . .

I am thankful for people like this, for they make the world more livable, Their spirit of service is summed up in these little words . . . and then some.

— Carl Holmes

The verse talks about three little words that are the secret to success in customer service and in life — *and then some*. The poem speaks about thoughtfulness, consideration, and kindness as part of *and then some* service. This phrase brings to mind Dave, our friendly dry cleaner counterman. When you visit this business, Dave greets you with a smile, has your telephone number memorized (so he can put it in the computer to start your drop-off transaction), and asks about your week. Dave then carries out your clean laundry and carefully hangs it in your car. Dave recognizes the significance of making each customer feel important. He —

Smiles and acknowledges each customer the moment she steps in the store
- Makes the customer feel welcome
- Increases his chance for a better customer encounter
- Improves his voice tone

Remembers his customers' telephone numbers and uses his customers' names
- Makes the customer feel important
- Brings the encounter to a more personal level
- Develops long-term business relationships and customer loyalty

Shows interest in each customer
- Connects on events happening in his customers' lives
- Makes the customer feel special
- Entices the customer to return

Since *and then some* service requires being thoughtful of others, considerate, and kind, another area of customer service comes to mind. There comes a time in serving others when the answer to their request is "no." But even though the answer is "no," there is still a way to use *and then some* service. I have developed an *and then some* service way of saying "no" to someone — the Compassionate No. A friend once told me of a service encounter she had. She asked a salesperson to do something for her. After a much heated debate, the salesperson asked abruptly what letter of no she didn't understand. Wow, that salesperson surely was having a bad service day.

Dorothy illustrates the Compassionate No technique day in and day out as she works in a call center for a new medication trial. Her job is to process callers requesting to be put in the trial program. Many times her answer to the caller's request is no, but time and time again Dorothy says no in a way that makes a difference to her callers. She listens to their plights, responds with an empathetic reply, gives them additional contacts when she can, and concludes with phrases that show she cares. Many times Dorothy ends her conversations with, "I wish I could do more for you."

Look how the Compassionate No technique aligns itself with *and then some* service.

Put yourself in the customer's place
- Address the emotional part of the request
- Remain empathetic

Talk less, listen more
- Listen with your ears, eyes, and heart
- Hear the full request

Use phrases that elicit the customer's understanding
- "I wish I could do more."
- "I hope you can understand our position."

Another example of *and then some* service is shown in something I've labeled contagious enthusiasm. The "E factor," as many of us refer to it, has been given much publicity lately. Researchers have documented that enthusiasm is often the distinguishing factor in being hired for a job, receiving a promotion, standing out among the crowd, or being viewed as approachable. What is fascinating about enthusiasm is that it can be caught from others without realizing it.

To view contagious enthusiasm in full, let's take a look at Alexis's experience on her bus ride from the airport terminal to the long-term parking lot. Alexis arrived at Philadelphia International Airport at 6 a.m.; she had taken the red eye in from the west coast. As the bus pulled up to the curb to pick up its passengers, Tom, the bus driver, greeted each person with a smile and an enthusiastic, "Good Morning; Welcome to Philadelphia!" As Tom drove from pick-up point to pick-up point, he exchanged interesting tidbits about the city. Furthermore, he jumped out of his seat to help men and women with their heavy luggage. By the time passengers were ready to be dropped off at their parking points, most were showing signs of contagious enthusiasm to meet their day.

Since Alexis was the last one off the bus, she asked Tom what gave him such enthusiasm for his work. His answer remains with Alexis today.

"I treat each day as a prized possession;
I treat each day with great respect; and
I appreciate the day, my tasks, and the people I meet."

Tom's answer aligns itself perfectly with *and then some* service. Carl Holmes' poem states that *and then some* people meet their obligations and responsibilities fairly and squarely, *and then some.* That is exactly what Tom's way of service illustrates. Can you imagine the change in people if they approached their days with similar sentiments?

Another *and then some* service opportunity surfaces when you are unsure of an answer to a question. *And then some* service in this case is — When In Doubt, Find Out. A way for you to convey this to the customer is to say, "I want to be sure I am giving you accurate, up-to-date information, so let me check with someone." Finding out what you don't know doesn't mean you are inadequate. It means you are willing to learn and add new information to your knowledge bank.

Take a look at this example, and see if you can relate to it. This situation was a real eye opener for me. It was the first day of graduate school, and we were assigned our first major project by Dr. Alexander. As he explained what he expected, my mind whirled with questions. When he asked if anyone had any questions, not a soul among those fourteen strangers raised her hand. "Wait a minute!" I thought. I had five or six questions to ask; so I asked them. Still not another person spoke up. At that point I seriously doubted my scholastic ability and my belonging in this class. I pondered whether or not I was too old or too out of touch with the field to be pursuing an advanced degree.

What happened next quickly changed my mind. I decided to conduct an informal survey during our break. I asked the first person, "Did you know what Dr. Alexander expected?" "No, I was glad you asked." The next person, "Did you know what Dr. Alexander expected?" "No, I was glad you asked." This went on for the next three classmates I approached. Not one was willing to take the risk and admit uncertainty about what was expected. From that moment on I encouraged people around me — when in doubt, find out!

If you look around, you'll find *and then some* service cropping up in all industries and professions. Recently, a local hospital unveiled a first-of-its-kind facility — a hospital whose goal is to take care of its patients, not only from a clinical perspective, but from a personal point-of-view as well. How?

Instead of using volunteers to meet and greet patients, this hospital has hired full-time paid employees in the nursing units under the title of customer service representatives. These CSRs are on-call for any non-medical needs patients and their families may have to make their stay less stressful and more pleasant. CSRs tend to the personal side of a hospital stay by providing attention to a patient's non-medical needs. The CSRs are equipped with cellular phones, and they give out their phone numbers to their patients. The patients are told to call their CSR for any reason.

This program raises the bar for patient treatment beyond medical procedures. It ensures that patients feel they are more than just a bed and a room number. *And then some* service is evident from the moment the

patient enters the hospital; the CSRs

- Greet patients entering the hospital
- Give patients their telephone number and a helping hand
- Escort patients to tests
- Help patients order from cafeteria menus
- Provide a listening ear
- Hold a scared hand
- Look for ways to make the patient's stay more comfortable
- Fulfill the needs of the patient's family

Patients and families are already singing praises about this service, and the hospital is sure the program will be emulated quickly by other hospitals.

During my programs, time and time again participants share their best customer service encounters, encounters that stand out above the rest. Following are just a few of my favorites.

First, there is Russ's *and then some* encounter. Russ needed to change dentists after being with the same dentist for over ten years. If you are like most people, changing dentists can be an uncomfortable experience. Luckily Russ chose Dr. Brandon, a dentist who demonstrated *and then some* service.

Russ scheduled his yearly checkup with Dr. Brandon. During the checkup the X-ray indicated that a filling needed replacing. Since another patient had cancelled her appointment that morning, Dr. Brandon asked Russ if he would like to have the filling replaced while the dentist had the time available. Russ hesitated for a moment but then agreed. The filling was replaced and Russ was on his way.

What occurred that evening was a true sign of *and then some* service. Around eight the phone rang at Russ's home. Lo and behold, it was Dr. Brandon inquiring about any discomfort Russ might be having. Wow — his dentist displayed *and then some* service, which in turn made

Russ feel he had made a good choice by selecting Dr. Brandon.

The following service encounter involves a profession that usually takes a bum rap. It took place in a busy courtroom. Beverly was in court with her attorney on a minor traffic violation. As she and her attorney sat waiting for her case to be called, Beverly witnessed the compassionate side of *and then some* service.

Another defendant was appearing before the court without any legal representation. The judge was scolding the defendant because she had not appeared on previous court dates. Beverly's attorney recognized the limited mental capacity of the defendant. Without a moment's hesitation, he stood up, introduced himself to the court, and proceeded to stand in *pro bono* to represent the other defendant.

Finally, let's take a look at Kimberly's encounter. When two of her tires were slashed at a local club, Kimberly called her local Firestone store to ask about replacements. Jeff answered the phone with sunshine in his voice. After realizing the tires she needed were not in stock, Jeff promised to get back to Kimberly once he located the tires. Sure enough, Jeff called back with the good news; he had located the replacement tires. What happened next is classic *and then some* service.

The following day Jeff went on his lunch hour to pick up the tires, so they could be replaced that afternoon. Jeff recognized how stressful the ordeal had been to Kimberly and wanted to hasten the solution. When Kimberly arrived to pick up her car, she said it was easy to recognize Jeff among the other employees at the facility; he was the one with a spring in his walk and a smile on his face.

You will recall the beginning of this chapter when I stated that *and then some* service is not about being miles ahead of others to be recognized as superior at what we do. We only need to give, *and then some*, which sometimes is just a half-inch more.

Start looking around for others who live the spirit of Carl Holmes' wonderful poem, "And Then Some." You, too, will be pleasantly surprised how many others have not only made it their model of service but their way of life!

ABOUT CAROL A. KIVLER

Carol Kivler is president of Kivler Communications, a consulting firm that works with individuals and teams to develop fine-tuned verbal and written communication skills, which lead to improved results. Whether Carol is providing one-on-one coaching, leading a seminar, or delivering a keynote, individuals are intrigued by her unique learning environment. She has been coined, "Cheerleader to Your Soul," by audiences. Carol has made a difference in companies such as American Express, The New York Times Broadcasting Group, Federal Reserve Bank, Ernst & Young, Janssen, Pharmaceutica, and Yale Manufacturing. Carol holds a master's from Fordham University in human resource education and a bachelor's from the College of New Jersey in business education. She has taught both in secondary and higher education settings. She is a member of the National Speakers Association, the American Association of Trainers and Developers, and the Office Advisory Council of Mercer County Community College.

Contact Information:
Carol A. Kivler
Kivler Communications
8 Hart Court
Titusville, NJ 08560
Phone: (609) 737-8157
Fax: (609) 737-8812
E-mail: kivlercom@worldnet.att.net
Website: www.kivlercom.com

SERVICE TO YOUR NUMBER ONE CUSTOMER

by Pat Veal

We live during a time when customer service is of the utmost importance. How we serve has become as important as what we serve and whom we serve. Customer service can be a determinant of business success.

Think about it. We enter a restaurant. The hostess seats us. We sit at a table that has just been cleared by a bus person. A waiter or waitress takes our order. The cooks prepare it. The server brings it to the table. We expect everyone in that chain to provide good customer service. And it is also mandatory that they provide each other good customer service for the experience to be enjoyable. Would our experience be very pleasant if our waiter yelled at the chef? Probably not.

As we consider customer service, we usually place our customers somewhere in the external. The degree to which we serve them is directly proportional to our perception of their value to us.

Occasionally we expand our definition of customer service to include internal customers as well, those fellow team members who contribute as service providers to the same external customers that we serve. We soon discover the value in providing good internal customer service. As we acknowledge our internal customers and give good customer service, we create a healthy, harmonious, productive environment. As we increase productivity, we increase profit.

To maximize productivity it is necessary to step outside our current belief system and include our number one customer, the one who has been with us longest, the one who will be with us to the end, the one whom we see early in the morning and late at night, the one who looks at us as we look into the mirror, ourselves. Without proper self-treatment, we are short changing our other customers, cheating them out of the best. But this is not deliberate. Many of us just don't know any better, for surely if we knew better, we would do better. There are as many excuses for not taking time for ourselves as there are days in the year from, "I don't have time," to "I don't need all that stuff," to "I'm afraid," to "I can't afford to." Well you can't afford not to. We will examine how to serve ourselves through thoughts, words, and actions.

Thoughts are the molds that shape our words and actions. They are the foundation that determines the direction of our experience. Everything begins as a thought. Some thoughts are brief, fleeting even, like mosquito bites. Many times we don't notice the little needle-nose critter has paid us a visit until we see physical evidence as a red, itchy, bump on our once smooth skin.

An African proverb tells us not to look where we fell, but to look where we slipped. That takes us back to our thoughts. Before the mistake was an action, it was a thought. Consider the following as you prepare for your attitude tune-up or complete overhaul.

Love Yourself: Self-love is something more people would claim than not, but to some it is a foreign concept. Self-love is paramount in self-service. We must love ourselves even when we aren't acting lovable. We can receive a good lesson on self-love if we just observe babies. They see themselves in a mirror and express joy, for they see only beauty.

Accept Yourself: An extension of self-love is self-acceptance. We must accept ourselves as unique, unrepeatable expressions in the universe. Even if we don't accept some behavior, we understand that we are still in a period of growth.

Forgive Yourself: As we are each having a human experience, we are bound to make mistakes. As quickly as we make a mistake is how quickly we should forgive ourselves.

Know Yourself: If you know who you are and whose you are, where you are is understood to be a place where there are opportunities to learn.

Hold Positive Thoughts: Like begets like. Holding to positive thoughts creates positive outcomes.

Change Your Thoughts: Life is a series of transitions. Always reserve the right to change your opinion based on enlightenment. Remember, we always have choices. That is what growth is all about.

Think for Yourself: Appoint you as designated thinker, at least for yourself. Understand there is no shortage of unsolicited, volunteer, armchair quarterbacks for your life. Relieve them of their duties and take charge of your destiny by thinking for yourself and creating your own life.

Give Yourself Permission to Disagree With Another Person: In any relationship, there are bound to be disagreements and not only is that okay, it is healthy. It keeps the mind active and in good working condition.

Let Go of Fear: Fear is one of the biggest barriers to success. And most often the thing we fear is only an illusion, a molehill that we blow up to mountainous proportions. Most of the time the things that we fear never happen.

We should not allow fear of the unknown to prevent us from treading on new ground, going places where nobody has been, trying something new. Thank God, that incorporated into the power of choice, is the option to change. And there are no rules, such as you have to stick with a decision until the cock crows four times, nor is there a lifetime limit of 2567 times per family. We have the freedom to try something new and reserve our right to try something else if we so desire. Dare to be different. After all, if everybody tried to milk the same cow, somebody would not drink milk.

Be Slow to Anger: Whoever created the phrase, "fight fire with fire," was not a firefighter. Have you ever seen firefighters responding to a three-alarm fire in fire trucks, with ladders and *fire* hoses? Of course not! Fighting fire with fire just creates more fire, more destruction. To put out a fire, you need water. Sometimes we have to just let the fire burn out. You know that person intent on arguing? Sometimes it is good just to let him argue, alone. Occasionally just a little bit of anger can be a catalyst to taking action but anger usually does more harm than good. Anger can also create side effects that we don't want, such as a rise in our blood pressure or blood sugar, headaches or a severe loss of hair. When at all possible (and that is always) lose the anger.

Out of the heart, the mind speaks. The mouth is the vessel through which the words come. As we become more health conscious, we may fast to flush our system and rid our bodies of toxins, after which we change habits to stay clean. We can apply the same principles to our verbiage. Some words and phrases we have outgrown and they should no longer be a part of our vocabulary. How can we use words effectively for our own customer service?

Speak With Power: Words have power. Words of a lion spoken with the voice of a mouse are ineffective. Your words must convince your listeners of their validity starting with yourself. Credibility is important. If you say, "I am healthy, wealthy, whole, and free" just above a whisper through chattering teeth, you will convince your audience of nothing.

Speak Words of Prosperity: Choose your words carefully so that they always support the prosperity concept. Remember, too, that while prosperity includes, it is not limited to, financial abundance. Someone who continually cries "broke" or continually threatens to dribble (bounce) a check to the bank often can't understand why his or her account balance frequently approaches zero. As you stake your prosperity claim, include perfect health, good relationships and plenty of time.

Speak Truth: It is the truth that sets us free. To speak the truth, we must know the truth. Maybe some study time is in order.

Speak Positive, Uplifting Words: From the moment that they leave our lips, words move through the universe to accomplish what we sent them out to do. Sometimes, while we are getting our thoughts properly aligned, we have to harness and maybe even muzzle our words or they can act like fire-breathing dragons and burn up everything in their path.

Avoid Gossip: Gossip is one of the most destructive forces around. Feelings have been hurt and lives ruined by an unfounded statement, blown out of proportion and spread like wild fire. But gossip does not travel where it is not welcome. Take up the welcome mat, now.

Speak Up: Speak with conviction. We all should have some principles that are not available for compromise. Integrity is important.

Speak Lovingly: As we love ourselves, we must remember to speak lovingly to ourselves and about ourselves. We can be our own worst critics if we aren't careful. The next time you look at yourself in a group picture, rather than notice your hair out of place or how much weight you've gained, see your beautiful smile.

Silence Is Okay: There is value in silence. In silence is our strength. It is during silence that we are able to listen and to hear.

Learn to Say No Sometimes: Is it difficult for you to tell people no? Do you feel tired, run down, and worn out? Would you rather avoid people than admit that you don't want to do something? Have you ever done something that you didn't want to do and been angry with yourself afterwards? Do you make up excuses for not doing something? Stop wearing yourself down! It is okay to say no, and no is a complete sentence.

Actions, like words, are evidence of our thoughts. Sometimes we know that a change in behavior is necessary. We can use our human will and physical ability to change our behavior. Sometimes we must fake it until we make it. Unless there is an accompanying change in thought process, however, the behavior modification is only temporary. As we change our thoughts, our actions change automatically. We can and should nurture ourselves through our actions. Try some of the following:

Be Kind to Yourself: Are there things that you would like to do, yet you sit around waiting for someone to do them for you? Are you hoping that next Valentine's Day or on your next birthday you'll get what you want if she will just buy it or he will take you there? When is the last time you did something nice for you? Why wait for someone else to do it? You're worth it, aren't you?

Be Patient With Yourself: How many times have we heard the cliché, Rome wasn't built in a day? We apply that cliché to all kinds of situations and experiences that call for patience. We deserve the same degree of experiences that call for patience. We deserve the same degree of patience that we offer to others. It's okay if we don't make a home run every time we swing at the ball. In fact, sometimes we will strike out and that's okay too. What's important is, when it's our turn to bat again, we step up to the plate again.

Forgive Yourself: If you fall down, get up. If you fall down again, get up again. If you make a mistake, learn the lesson, forgive yourself, and move on.

Take Time to Rest: It takes someone who feels overworked to understand the value of rest. Children don't want to take a nap for fear they may miss out on something. Adults feel there is too much to do and may not get adequate rest. As stress-related conditions surface, periods of rest are most needed and appreciated. By now we should be claiming an abundance of time and, with that abundance, using some of it for rest.

Take Time to Play: Everything that we did in the classroom has a purpose in the school of life. Our class curriculum consisted of the basics of reading, writing, and arithmetic; it also included recess. We had an opportunity to separate ourselves from the pressures of school-work and spend time enjoying recreation. That added balance. We need that same balance today. They told us then all work and no play makes Jack a dull boy. They were right.

Take Time to Pray: Upon rising . . . pray! Before retiring. . . pray! It makes a difference in your days and your nights and in you!

Learn Something: Life is not a spectator sport. It would be great if we could observe some portions over a big screen television or as a power point presentation complete with sound, animation, and graphics. We could armchair quarterback to our hearts' content, always knowing the best play. We could double click and open a new page at will or click undo and act as though our last action did not happen. But life in all its glory is not like that. It is a journey complete with possibilities, including hills, valleys, deep turns, bad weather, flat tires, and running hot. It also has sunshine, cool breezes, beautiful scenery, majestic mountains, beaches, sunrises, sunsets, stars, and nature-painted canvases. Life with all its splendor is full of lessons. As we are open and receptive, we learn and we grow. Experience is the best teacher.

Take Time to Laugh: Allow laughter to flow freely in your life. Laughter is healing. And the best object of your laughter is yourself. When you can recognize the folly in your own antics, you have arrived.

Spend Time With Family and Friends: Too often we downplay the importance of loved ones. Start right now to allot some of your abundance of time to them.

Love Your Work: We should love what we do. That attitude alone removes the feeling of burden from it. If we understand that we have been selected to perform a service that no one can do like us, we realize how special we are. As we lovingly and proudly perform the service that we have been assigned, we will see all of our needs met and our desires fulfilled.

As we complete this chapter, I challenge you to form a corporation. Name it TWA, Inc. Your partners are **T**houghts, **W**ords, and **A**ctions. This is a powerful partnership and through it you can accomplish whatever you choose. And live each day as though it were your best (not as your last). We don't know the day or hour of our last day, but if we get the best out of each day, when our last one arrives, it is our best.

Pop Quiz *(to see if you paid attention)*

1. Your relative has asked you to baby sit and you don't want to. Do you
   - a. baby sit anyway
   - b. pretend you have plans
   - c. use caller ID to screen your calls for a month
   - d. say no

2. You interview for a job and someone else is hired. Do you
   - a. kick, cry and scream
   - b. contact an attorney
   - c. decide you'll never get a job
   - d. realize that it wasn't for you

3. You see a pile of dog poop on the sidewalk ahead. Do you
   - a. rush ahead and step in it
   - b. find out who did it
   - c. call the police
   - d. walk around it

4. At the bank, the teller makes a rude remark to you. Do you
   - a. punch her/him in the nose right then and there
   - b. wait outside for the teller to get off from work
   - c. demand they be fired on the spot
   - d. ignore it, knowing the remark is not true

   If you answered "d" to all of the above, congratulations!

ABOUT PAT VEAL

Working with the Georgia Department of Labor as an Employer Marketing Representative, Pat Veal has first-hand experience connecting job seekers and job opportunities. In her job search workshops she helps people identify their true skills, structure resumés that stand out from the crowd, and prepare for important interviews. She also coaches people in employer expectations, job retention, and how to maintain a winning attitude. Pat educates employers as well with up-to-the-minute information on tax credits, federal bonding, and recruitment consulting. Pat is also an ordained minister with a universal message of love, peace, and trust. Her training translates into different "languages" for different audiences including corporate, government, religious, spiritual, youth, addicted and others. Pat reaches diverse populations with her motivational, inspirational, and joyful messages.

Contact Information:
Pat Veal
E-mail: PVeal1@bellsouth.net

"INSIDE THE BOX"
CUSTOMER SERVICE

by John Kennedy

I t all started about a year ago when my wife opened her own consignment shop in our hometown of Sykesville, Maryland. In order to create an inventory for the customers, we had to go out and find items that people wanted to get rid of and create an instantly full shop.

Her business partner's parents had occupied the same home for thirty-five years, and when that happens, you collect a lot of stuff. So off to Philadelphia we went.

My sole responsibility in the journey was to watch our one-year-old son, Benjamin . . . easy enough, I thought. While the shop owners were rummaging through box after box after box of old collectibles, I happened to find a box of baseball souvenirs — in particular, one with Brookes Robinson memorabilia inside. He just happens to be my favorite baseball player of all time.

So I started to browse through the box for a couple of minutes and quickly lost track of my boy Ben. In a small panic and slight amount of fear, I began searching for him in all the usual places — up the stairs, behind the doors, in other rooms. About two minutes passed, which seemed like an eternity, and after calling his name several times, it became clear to me I was in big trouble. One assignment for the whole trip blown over a few Brookes Robinson items. I decided to call his name one more time before we assembled a search party, and in a con-cerned, yet playful voice, I said "Ben?" I heard a quiet "Da" (which translates to "Dad" from a one-year-old). I said his name again to try to locate him and he again responded "Da?" I finally discovered him just where I began looking for him. He was underneath one of the empty boxes and was waiting for me to find him. I searched everywhere for my son outside of the box when all I needed to do was look "inside the box." I come from a long history of customer service in the hospitality industry. Restaurants and hotels are where I spent roughly fifteen years as a busboy, waiter, manager, director, and finally general manager. One of my most memorable experiences with a great leader was in my job as a director of sales in a busy hotel in the Washington, D.C. area. I had the good fortune of working with a gentleman named Bill Mitchell. On my first day of work, we met to discuss his expectations. I had read that if you meet a new manager, you should ask what his or her "super objective" is. The "super objective" is the one area where you should concentrate your energies (reports, clear communications, teamwork, customer service). His response was that I was to "make some beds." That was not exactly what I was expecting to hear. I was hired as a director of sales; my job was to put "heads in beds," not make them.

I trusted his idea, and proceeded to make my first bed two days later with the help of one of our housekeepers, Edna (you never forget your first bed!). After completing the assignment, I figured I was done with making beds and proceeded with the job at hand — "putting heads in beds."

Mr. Mitchell checked in a few days later to see how I was getting along and I told him fine.

He asked if I had made any beds, and I informed him of the "wonderful" experience with Edna days before.

He said, "Great, make ten more."

I responded, "Is this some sort of hotel hazing I am not familiar with?"

He laughed, and left, and left me to laugh about his management style. The laughter lessened when I realized what he wanted me to learn.

When it comes time to enhance our customer service, to create an environment where customers are heard and helped, who is closest to the customer on a daily basis in a hotel? The housekeepers! How often are they asked how we can improve our ability to meet and exceed expectations on a daily basis? Not often enough!

I strongly believe that some of the most creative ideas are housed in the heads of those we manage and work with every day. Unfortunately, we may neglect to tap into the internal customer within our own organizations. We may ask for their input, but merely asking does not mean they will offer their ideas. The challenge in our work force is to create an environment where idea sharing, creativity, customer service and success are grown "inside the box."

Humans are fairly simple, and we have four simple human needs.

Our first need is to feel *welcome*.

My challenge to you is to create an environment where your internal customers feel welcome when they arrive at work. A simple "hello" goes a long way. A sincere smile, a thank you for a job well done, or a personal note. Often, managers in a customer service environment are under great pressure in dealing with difficult customers, scheduling, multiple tasks, multiple personalities, training, family and everything else that goes with the territory of management, that they forget to "put deposits in the bank accounts" of those whom we manage. That concept is from the *7 Habits of Highly Effective People* by Dr. Steven Covey. It is best said . . . continue to put money in the accounts of your internal customers, and they are more likely to return it to the account of the company by the service they give.

The second human need we have is to feel is *comfortable*.

If the environment in which your employees work is not one of comfort, you can be sure that the service they provide to your "external customers" will not be comfortable either. Comfort is expressed in many ways: body language, tone of voice, and selection of words. If these three methods of communication are not in concert, the feeling of comfort is lost.

I arrived at a hotel one night somewhat late and was greeted by the front desk person who was slumped over the counter. Her first words were, "Can I help you?" Although her words were encouraging, her body language and tone of voice made me hear this — "I hate my job, you're part of my job, you do the math!"

Often, we attempt to put deposits in the accounts of our employees, but the message is lost by our body language and voice.

"Hey Sam, great job with that customer on the phone. I could tell the person was annoyed, and you handled it like a pro! Keep up the good work." We use the correct words; however, we are walking quickly by on the way to a meeting and the impression the employee gets is of a "drive-by schmoozing!" Take the time to put as much money in the account as you can with body, voice and words, and you will create a more comfortable environment at work.

The third human need is to feel *understood*.

I have two daughters, ages 11 and 12. If I had a dollar for every time they have said "I don't understand," I could retire tomorrow. In fact, a lack of understanding is usually the basis of most conflict with our customers — internally or externally. How many times have we said, "Oh, I didn't understand you meant that."

I had an employee in our sales office years ago who was a challenge to work with. Her work had slowed and her attitude had become somewhat negative, affecting the way she dealt with customers both internally and externally. She was single and played the field. On Mondays, she came to work with stories of her weekend dalliances, and shared them with the office. My only question to her was, "Where did your gentlemen caller take you to dinner?" (I could tell a quality catch by his choice of restaurant.) One of her dates had taken her to Vacarros, an outstanding Italian restaurant in the Little Italy area of Baltimore. When I heard that, I gave him two thumbs up! I asked her what she had liked most about the dinner, and she responded "the cannoli."

I made a mental note that Jen liked cannoli from Vacarro's and went on with my day. A few months later my wife and I went to Little Italy and had an enjoyable dinner. I remembered that Jen enjoyed cannoli (especially from Vacarro's) so we went there for dessert, and they were outstanding! I thought it would be a nice gesture to take some into work on Monday, so on that Saturday night, we boxed up three cannoli to go and went home.

On Sunday, I became hungry in the late afternoon, and was tempted to dig into the dessert from the night before. It was a great challenge to follow through on the original idea of giving all three to Jen; it was a battle of will against hunger. On Monday morning I grabbed the box with two cannoli and went to work.

I arrived before Jen and left the box on her desk with a note that read "breakfast of champions." The box had a Vacarro's label on it and when she arrived, she looked at the box with a strange expression, opened it, looked at me and asked, "You remembered that?"

I responded, "Yes."

She said "Did you go all the way there just for me?"

I responded "Well, we were around the corner from Vacarro's and remembered you enjoyed the cannoli, so we picked you up a couple" (actually three, but what she doesn't know won't hurt her).

I must tell you that on that day, our relationship changed from manager/employee to two people working as a team. I refer to this as the "Cannoli Factor" in my management presentations. I believe that all employees have a need to be understood, but they are different in what makes them feel that way. I challenge you to determine the "Cannoli Factor" in each of your employees. I am confident you will find a more positive environment to work in when every employee feels *welcome*, *comfortable*, and *understood*.

And the last human need is to feel *important*.

Employees want to be involved in what is happening in the work environment. Statistics show that the main reason for employees to leave a company is that they never felt they were an important part of the organization. Having their ideas listened to, having their opinions carry weight, having their creativity and innovation rewarded and recognized are incredible motivators.

Employees are usually the ones fighting the battle on the front lines, they are closest to the action, and they can contribute ideas that will create a more fulfilling, profitable, and customer-centric environment.

It is the responsibility of the leader/manager to create an environment in which employees, our internal customers, feel *welcome, comfortable, understood,* and *important.* The easiest way to accomplish those four needs . . . we have to make a couple of beds.

At a time where the distance between management and employees has grown farther and farther apart, you will find a morale-starved, "not my job" mentality among many customer service representatives. They are usually paid less than their value to the company, are usually on the receiving end of anger and grief daily, and sometimes may not receive the support they need from their managers.

In the most successful customer-centric environments, that distance is collapsed to the same level, managers are not afraid to get their hands dirty, and the value of employee input is held in high esteem. This chapter has been dedicated to utilizing the talents, ideas, innovations, energy, enthusiasm, and expertise of your internal customers — your employees — the folks who think *"Inside the Box!"*

ABOUT JOHN KENNEDY

*A*udiences in North America, Europe and Australia have felt empowered by John Kennedy's keynote speeches and seminars to shake it up!
*His expertise, insight, and energetic delivery style have positioned him as a
speaker of choice for progressive, global companies and associations such
as Taco Bell, General Electric, Marriott Hotels, American Bus Association,
Society of Government Meeting Professionals, and Elizabeth Arden. John
focuses his presentations on key issues in customer service, management,
and leadership, especially in the service-related industries of hospitality
and technology. He combines creativity, research, writing and fifteen years of
management and sales experience to create a powerful, dynamic, and insightful presentation. He is the author of the book* Management That Cooks.

Contact Information:
John Kennedy
Kennedy Consulting
2634 Old Washington Road
Westminster, MD 21157
Phone: (410) 751-8838
Fax: (410) 751-9419
E-mail: john@ishakeitup.com
Website: www.ishakeitup.com

PARDON ME DEAR...
I Believe You May Have Forgotten Which Side of the Counter You Are On

by Jae Pierce-Baba

I t doesn't matter how nice, bright, or well educated you are; being angry, hurt, or disappointed over a customer service issue blocks your good judgment, no matter which side of the counter you may find yourself on.

Being angry with yourself or with others at times is part of human nature, but scientific studies prove that staying angry and indulging in self-righteous outrage take a huge negative toll on our mental and physical health. Anger increases our pulse rate and blood pressure and stresses our immune system. Resentment over a customer service issue undermines your ability to think clearly and feel calm.

My personal challenge to you, the reader, is to develop the habit of using humor as a survival strategy for life. Humor replaces expected outcomes with the unexpected.

Look for the humor in adversity. When in the company of a difficult person, do self-affirmations of "I *will* find humor in this situation!" Stressful situations can turn into great storytelling experiences, so why wait — assess the humor potential as it happens!

I recently had to make this humor commitment to myself. I was shopping at a large national home improvement chain to price a water heater for a charity project I was involved in. I realized I needed to phone the director to ask what the budget allowance for the purchase was. The customer service area was nearby. I strolled over to the desk, and a gum-popping, hair-twisting, and accessory-fiddling teen-age clerk named Amber greeted me. She just stared at me until I asked to see the phone book.

"You will have to go to customer service desk 2," she replied.

"Where is that?" I asked.

She mutely pointed to the desk six inches directly to my left — I sidestepped six inches to the left and waited. Amber moved six inches to her right, standing in front of me at the second desk, and completely serious she said, "Yes?" as if she had never seen me before.

"The phone book!" I semi-screamed — not knowing whether to laugh or cry.

She signed deeply, folded her arms across her chest, looked at me with bored and sullen eyes, her bright red lips pursed nastily, and said, "We don't have any phone books."

I looked up and down and all around: "Okay, where are the cameras?" "Where is the crew for *America's Funniest Customer Service Bloopers*?" I looked at Amber and said, "This is a joke, right?" She looked directly at me, arched her brows, rolled her eyes, and started to turn away.

I leaned forward against the counter, and in a sweet voice, the words of my Gramma Bessie came out of my mouth, *"Pardon me, dear, but I believe you may have forgotten which side of the counter you are on!"*

The quizzical expression on her face was the laugh I needed to get a new perspective on things — and as I went out that door I left the frustration and emotional upset behind me.

Unfortunately, anger is a form of entertainment for many humans — worldwide wrestling, extreme action movies, television "reality" shows, political radio talk shows — all feature conflict and confrontation. A recent study that researched a wide variety of industries reports that physical violence has occurred in their workplace. In the same study, 42 percent say they have been subjected to verbal abuse on the job and 29 percent admit they have shouted at a co-worker.

Widespread rudeness is reflected in people's misuse of technology; intrusive cell phone conversations, obsessive self-isolating computer use, using e-mail to avoid face-to-face contact, anonymous chat room psuedo-relationships, and compulsive use of the Internet. None of this technology is harmful, but our misuse of it reduces our ability to interact with others — an inability that is easily evident in poor customer service.

Using Humor as a Power Tool for Sales and Customer Service

Laughing with others builds confidence, brings people together, and lets us express amusement at common predicaments. Good communication leads to more efficient methods of problem solving by encouraging us to bond and share ideas. Humor works by creating cooperation between people. Companies are increasingly hiring humor consultants to help reduce employee stress and burnout. Executives are seeing humor as an effective way to relieve tension, build morale, and bring a new and creative perspective to serious challenges. Humor builds communication quickly, it is free, legal, has no side effects, you can't overdose on it, and it is cheaper than Prozac. If you can laugh about potentially stressful situations, you are in control. Research indicates that a laugh is a powerful listening tool, learning device, icebreaker, self-healer, attention grabber, and a forceful selling tool.

Signs of humor are as unique as a human thumbprint and can range from a slight raise of the eyebrows to laughing out loud until your sides ache and tears run down your face. We don't need scientists to tell us laughter makes us feel good — we just know it does! On a day-to-day basis, you're not going to be wearing wacky glasses on your face or have a whoopee cushion attached to your body, so start looking at life with a more lighthearted perspective.

When you are in a stressful customer service situation, your use of humor starts as an inner attitude. Imagine irritated persons speaking to you in their underwear, or visualize a big red clown nose on their faces. Instead of a snarl, you may actually wear a smile — even in difficult situations!

The Channels for Successful Business Communication

Being connected with another human being is the first step in having a meaningful conversation. It is crucial that during a business related situation, you enter and exit the conversation on personal common ground, e.g., "Hello, Jan, How are you doing? How is that new puppy? Please be at the meeting tomorrow at four to discuss the new policy changes, o.k.? See you tomorrow, Jan, and drive home carefully tonight." By entering and exiting her conversation with true personal affinity and reality for Jan, her colleague connected to her as a caring co-worker, but Jan also knew that she would be responsible for business as usual tomorrow.

When customers are welcomed by name or questions are asked about their families, pets, professions, or hobbies, they feel like part of an extended family. Everyone wants to feel personally connected to those they do business with. *This is the basis of customer service.*

Laughter changes our perspective: it alters the way we relate to what is happening to us, especially things that we don't have immediate control over (read LIFE). That is the healing part of laughter because humor shifts how we relate to events that occur everyday. It pulls us out of negative tunnel vision and fosters new and creative viewpoints with which to solve our problems.

Attitudes, viewpoints, and belief systems are keys to the way we react emotionally to the environment. According to Robert Provine, author of *Laughter; A Scientific Investigation*, we laugh to promote social bonding — a trigger that appears to be genetically determined. His studies document that humans actually laugh more frequently during the course of conversation at things that *aren't* funny to show agreement or approval than they do to voice their amusement at something that tickles their funnybone. Other studies suggest that people laugh 30 percent less when they are alone and 90 percent of the time people are laughing at nothing specific. Humor allows you to deal with a crisis in customer relations and then be able to face the next person calmly and with a smile.

Eye contact is a sign of both self-respect and mutual respect. It demonstrates that you are confident enough to look at the person who is speaking and that you are giving that person your undivided attention. Remember how good it felt the last time you felt truly listened to? When a person is thinking of a response instead of listening, there is a tendency to look down and away from the speaker. Listen instead, and making eye contact will be a natural reaction. If you look in people's eyes when they are talking, they will be much more responsive and enthusiastic. Need eye contact? Look at the center of the eyes or one eye to achieve and maintain contact. Just about everybody can relate to Zig Ziglar's statement, *"Most people do not communicate, they simply take turns talking."*

Working as a pediatric occupational therapist, I frequently discussed children and their therapy goals with their parents. My young patient Shannon had a goal of making eye contact with me for 30 seconds but was progressing slowly. I met with Shannon's mother at our first conference and quickly realized that she never made eye contact either — not once in the first fifteen minutes we were chatting. She was looking at the ground with such interest, I got on the floor, lay on my back with my face directly in her line of vision, and asked, "Do you understand what I am saying about your son?" I don't know if she was afraid of what I would do next, but for the next two years of Shannon's therapy, she made eye contact with me and we had clear and respectful communication. Simple, good eye contact was the starting point required for good communication to achieve our therapy goals for Shannon. This could be true in almost every customer service encounter. Customer service is doing the right thing in your job, even if the methods are somewhat unorthodox.

> *"If humor is accepted, you are probably in an environment where people are rewarded for the things they do, they are picked up after failures, and disagreements are settled more easily. If the humor level is down, that is probably also an indicator of how other things are settled."*
>
> — Richard Davidson,
> Management Consultant

The Humor Rule: The rule is, laughter leads to listening.

When someone laughs with you, he or she is giving indirect approval to you in the form of personal agreement. After you say something funny, whatever you say will have a much greater impact and be more memorable. After people laugh once, they expect and want to laugh again.

The Punch Line and the Bottom Line Do Intersect After Laughter:

- The prospect is listening and the seller is enjoying a productive relationship.

- Emotional moods are lighter, more positive, and optimistic.

- The prospect is more "in the mood" to buy because of the trust factor established with the seller.

- Fun or lightheartedness closes the gap between "professional" and "friendly" for both parties.

- A sense of humor gives you an edge on the competition because people are attracted to happy people.

What the Power of Humor
Can Do for You in Customer Service

Take time to promote laughter, starting by smiling daily. Serious people are frequently seen as distant, negative, arrogant, or intimidating; is that the image you want to project as you walk the halls *or* work in the malls?

Why is the Negaholic Virus so Contagious?

It seems that people are constantly on edge — ready to retaliate if they feel anyone is disrespecting them. What is behind all this aggression? I believe there are several reasons: the daily pace of life is moving faster and is more rushed; people feel a constant sense of urgency and emergency, which leads to stress and tension, and this creates a greater emotional distance between people. The result of the stress and tension is impatience and irritability, which cause people to go ballistic over trivial things. Humor brings people back into communication. It closes the gap and restores the human connection.

Customers are tolerant of problems they understand — *but they are not tolerant of being ignored.* For example, if an order can't be fulfilled immediately, protect customer goodwill by sending an acknowledgment letter or phone call promising fulfillment as soon as possible. Simple human courtesy is so uncommon and unexpected that it will create astonishing loyalty.

According to Anita Roddicks, owner of The Body Shop (in 37 countries), skillful employees are not the key to successful companies, and neither is money.

Ms. Roddicks believes great employees have these characteristics:

- Optimism
- Love
- Humanism
- Humor
- Enthusiasm
- Magic
- Intuition
- Fun
- Curiosity
- And the secret ingredient — euphoria

You can train people to do just about anything, but the key to real success in customer relations and motivated, long-term employees is hiring people who really *want* to do their jobs and who love to come to work. These cheerful people enliven the workplace and energize their co-workers. That is the difference having fun at work can make . . . for those on both sides of the counter.

15 Helpful Hints to Increase Your Laughter Factor

1. *Smile when you feel like frowning:* It takes 42 muscles to frown and 15 muscles to smile . . . so why work overtime? A smile is a universal symbol of being accepted. *Smile more:* we like to be around people who make us feel good, and we are drawn to those who relieve our tension, let us relax, and make us smile. Relaxation and feeling welcome inspire loyalty, and customer retention.

2. *Self-renewal:* Renewing yourself throughout the day with joy breaks will revive energy, restore creativity, change your perspective, and enhance strategic decision making. Re-energizing yourself is serious business and an essential survival strategy for getting from the rat race to relaxation.

3. *You don't have to be funny, just see funny:* Humor is an effective way to boost morale at work, connect with others on a heart-to-heart level, and communicate serious messages with a light touch. A good laugh does wonders for the energy level, and science-based research is proving that a sense of humor is a mature, life coping strategy that enables one to maintain a balanced perspective on life. Have fun by wearing funky socks, pins with humorous messages, hats that are unusual — fun is limited only by your own imagination.

4. *Journaling:* After a humorous experience, write down the details exactly, so that you can share it later with a friend and relive the fun all over again.

5. *Laughing out loud:* Laughter and associated positive emotions (joy, hope, faith, etc.) stimulate the body's natural defenses for optimal functioning. Solid science proves this; how we feel verifies it. People who respond to humor and appreciate the wit of others attract positive attention. Laughter tells those around you that you are a human being who enjoys a life filled with fun.

6. *Cultivate your sense of humor:* Laughter is a cathartic response that serves to cleanse the body of distressing emotions.

7. *Increase your comic vision:* Look for incompatible elements in everyday living. Humor is the ability to see the childlike element in everyday stressful situations. Humor happens in the moment — be ready to appreciate it!

8. *Don't be nasty:* Sarcasm literally means "to tear flesh." Humor at another's expense is risky in business. People may laugh at that

specific moment, but they may be left with a negative feeling about you.

9. *Laugh at yourself:* Laughing at yourself shows that you are down-to-earth and self-confident. Tell stories on yourself whenever appropriate. Laughing at yourself and exhibiting a sense of humor keep all aspects of life in perspective and take the edge off emotional or physical pain. Learn to laugh at what you do, without laughing at who you are. Laughter is a wonderful protector of mental and physical health!

10. *Keep a private internal joke with yourself:* A funny memory or actual event that only you know about can get you through some rough times.

11. *Do random acts of kindness:*
    - leave a dollar where someone will find it
    - sneak a candy bar in between papers to be filed
    - secretly pay for someone's coffee at a fast food place
    - compliment someone
    - smile at a stranger
    - let someone cut in front of you in traffic

12. *The joke's on the competition:* Try being dramatic, improvisational, silly. Your vibes will get others into the spirit of fun and give you an edge on the competition.

13. *Props:* Use small and funny toys, bumper stickers, yo yo's, bubbles, red noses or candy to encourage smiles.

14. *Joke Buddy:* Every week, pick a new joke and then exchange it with a specific person. That person should also have a new joke for you. Have a list of four jokes memorized with correct timing, set-up, and punch line.

15. *Using children as humor mentors in life:* Sounds of kids laughing and giggling are guaranteed to lift spirits. Children are spontaneous, eternally fascinated, and are totally absorbed in the present moment.

Communication and Customer Service:
Understanding the Basics

"If you lose a customer, you lose two ways.
One, you don't get their money and two, your competitors do."
— Bill Gates

I walked into the chichi dress shop on Michigan Avenue in Chicago, letting my eyes adjust to the cool atmosphere of bare wood, leather, chrome, and high prices. As I explored the racks of clothes, I realized that all the price tags had commas in them . . . Yikes! I browsed around but was not approached by any of the mannequin-like clerks all dressed in black like Johnny Cash.

Finally I asked about a gift item I thought came with a cosmetic purchase. The perky cosmetologist glanced at me with a look of disgust and said that *nothing* was free in her store. Embarrassed, I looked at her with a smile and nicely said, "Well, have a good day . . . oh! I see you have other plans!" It took all I had not to laugh out loud at the look on her face.

I left the store lighthearted and went and spent my money elsewhere.

Using the Funny Bone for Profit

Look at me. Talk to me. Answer my questions. Serve me.

Expectations, beliefs, attitudes, and values are communicated constantly through our words, facial expressions, posture, eye contact, voice tone and behavior. Be aware of your facial expressions, monitor your body language, exhibit enthusiasm, be approachable, and successful communication skills will be a natural part of your life. When people are truly listened to, they trust, and they buy into whatever it is you are selling — yourself, a product, or a viewpoint.

People who share humor at home or work tend to be more productive and more cooperative. The ability to be flexible in life may help deal with crisis situations as well as defuse anger or impatience.

Getting People to Listen:
Why God Gave Humans Two Ears and One Mouth

Listening is one of the most important elements in customer service. People spending their hard earned cash want to feel that their needs are being met and that their values are taken into consideration. This happens most quickly and assuredly when they are truly being listened to.

The object of any oral communication is to get people to listen and respond. Communication is two way; there's a time to talk and a time to listen. Are people listening and paying attention to your communications? Are you a good communicator? Do you understand the value given to the different areas of conversation? See how well you do on the following questions:

What percent do words affect communication? 7 percent!

What percent does voice tone affect communication? 40 percent!

What percent do non-verbal gestures affect communication?
53 percent!

Of this 53 percent, the gestures include facial expressions, body orientation (facing toward or facing away), eye contact, and conscious and unconscious gestures — looking at watch, pen, and body language, hair twirling, gazing off.

You can't reason with people who aren't paying attention to what you are saying.

Cracking Jokes, Not Skulls: Mirth in Management

Seen in a lumber yard: "We have less to fear from outside competition than from inside discourtesy, inefficiency and poor service."

Studies have shown that organizations that allow for lightening up in the workplace have less employee turnover, less employee downtime and less physical and emotional burnout. Research indicates burnout results from unabated stress and that stress is the basis of illness and disease. In today's society, we live in a constant state of stress, noise, trauma, and uncertainty. We are overwhelmed with negative input —

both personal and global. In our society, people suffer from "Hurry Sickness." Do you ever find yourself rushing to get somewhere and you don't even have to hurry? Well-placed humor can break the rush/haste cycle and create a different, less stressful perception of whatever situation is causing you stress: stuck in traffic, waiting in line, or a slow-moving person in front of you at the register.

When you keep a humorous perspective on daily life, you have an increased ability to keep anxiety/panic under control; emotional moods are lighter and more optimistic. Fun has been proven to be a vital component of an effective work environment. Many corporations are providing their employees with training in the value of humor and appropriate ways to have fun in the workplace.

Employees work faster and smarter when the organization allows for some loosening up. Great company motto: "If it isn't fun, we don't do it. If it's profitable and makes money, we make it fun." Be innovative in exceeding the customers' expectations by doing more than is required or expected, and customer retention will follow.

Author Tom Peters states: "The number one premise of business is that it need not be boring or dull. It ought to be fun. If it's not fun, you're wasting your life."

Corporations are slowly understanding the power of fun in the workplace. Ben and Jerry's has established a "Joy Committee." Nordstroms has live, classical piano music. The Seattle Fish Company entertains with fish throwing. What can you do to enliven your workplace?

A seven-year study done by author and educator C.W. Metcalf showed that in a work environment that encourages fun, employees have

- abundant energy   • greater self-esteem
- team spirit   • sustainable motivation
- positive attitudes

Being Fluid and Flexible — Essential Management Skills: Six Strategies for Tension Prevention

1. Breathe!

   - Use in stressful circumstances, difficult employee confrontations, negotiations, tough customers, and on roller-coaster rides.
   - In through nose and out through mouth: inhale to the count of four, and exhale to count of four.
   - Intentional breathing will slow you down.
   - Pace — slow; Depth — deep.
   - Inhale a vigorous double breath through the nostrils and exhale through the mouth with a AH-HA sound. Repeat three times.
   - Diaphramatic Breathing: Place one hand on your abdomen and the other on your chest. Emphasize the breathing of the abdomen, feeling the hand rise as you inhale and fall as you exhale. Let chest relax.

2. Get relaxed

   - Blessed are the flexible, for they shall not be bent out of shape!
   - Jaw and neck muscles tighten up when you are angry.
   - Avoid clenching jaw; let jaw go slack and open.
   - Focus on lengthening your neck muscles — put your right ear toward your right shoulder repeat on left side.
   - Go back to breathing technique.

3. Attitude Check

   - Surround yourself with funny, playful people.

> *"You can learn more about a person in an hour of play*
> *than in a year of conversation."*
>
> — Plato

- Don't take rude customer service personally.

- Be confident and self-assured, not arrogant.

- Do take others seriously; do not belittle them or their concerns.

- Don't take yourself too seriously! When you do, you increase your defensiveness and your aggravation.

- Create your own humor log/file.

- Utilize cartoons on memos, handouts, faxes, etc.

- Utilize electronic communication to receive or send uplifting comments or articles.

4. Scream

    When all else fails! Roll up the window in the car, get in a car wash, or wrap a towel around your head and let out a howl for joy. Screaming is a wonderful tension and anger release.

5. Be Present

    Learn to be appreciative of whatever you are currently doing. We spend entirely too much time thinking of the past and worrying about the future.

6. Count Your Blessings

    Stop and think about all the things that are going well in your life instead of focusing on what is wrong.

Motivation Is an Inside Job

There has never been a medical recorded case of anyone actually dying of laughter; in contrast, the term and implications of being "dead serious" are truly thought provoking!

If you feel exhausted after a good night's rest and *hate* to get up in the morning, then you may be in resistance to your life *as it is* and you need to take a critical look at what will make you happy. Being in resist-ance to your daily schedule may cause a feeling of depletion and fatigue. You are using all of your energy just to struggle through the day.

You will find that when you believe in your work and you are fol-lowing your heart, you will have the extra energy to make things happen.

As Garrison Keillor has said, "Humor is not a trick, not jokes. Humor is a presence in the world like grace and shines on everyone."

My wish for you is that the presence of humor, grace, and good customer service shine on you always, no matter which side of the counter you are on!

ABOUT JAE PIERCE-BABA

Jae Pierce-Baba has made it her mission to encourage others to lighten up in both personal and professional settings. Jae believes that laughing, humor and a sense of fun gives you an edge on the competition — from more easily selling your ideas and viewpoints to dealing serenely with cranky, irritable or stubborn people. In a world yearning for improved customer service, she believes a sense of humor is an essential life skill. Jae is founder and CEO of LipShtick Productions. She is a professional speaker, occupational therapist, comedienne, stage performer, writer, wife, and mother. She is an active member of The National Speakers Association and serves on several community boards of directors. Jae blends wit, compassion, and knowledge with a healthy dose of laugh-out-loud humor in her presentations. Audiences leave with smiles on their faces, good feelings in their hearts, and a clearer understanding of how to bring humor into their lives on a daily basis.

Contact Information:
Jae Pierce-Baba
LipShtick Productions
12206 Ridgepoint
Wichita, KS 56235
Phone: (316) 946-0422
Fax: (316) 946-0840
E-mail: jae@jaepierce-baba.com
Website: www.jaepierce-baba.com

THE DEADLY DOZEN: THE 12 DEADLY SINS OF CUSTOMER SERVICE

by Marian Madonia

There are 12 deadly sins of customer service. I call them the Deadly Dozen. Like a plague, they slowly kill our businesses. They are the result of our environment: a tough economy, limited resources, expecting employees to do more with less, a lack of compassion and caring, poor training or no training; the list goes on and on. We hear more and more about the importance of customer service, but it seems that many are focused only on filling the order and not the other services that are considered part of the deal. For example, when I buy a lawn mower at the hardware store, I am paying for the product (the lawnmower), but I am also buying someone who is helpful, knowledge-able, and sincere. People get the *letter* of customer service, but they don't get the *heart* of customer service. As a result, they commit one or more of the sins of customer service, *the Deadly Dozen:*

1. Refusing to Listen, Acknowledge, or Validate
2. Assumptions
3. Inconvenience/Treating the Customer as a Nuisance
4. Not Knowing Your Customer
5. Forgetting that Anyone is a Potential Customer
6. Arguing with Customers
7. Inefficiency
8. Lack of Integrity

9. Providing Incorrect or Inaccurate Information
10. Proving One's Self Right
11. Getting Even
12. Threats/Accusations

Refusing to Listen, Acknowledge, or Validate

About six months ago, I subscribed to one of the major anti-virus software services. I purchased the service on-line and had problems with it from the beginning. No matter what I did, I was unable to download the automatic upgrades for new viruses. It seemed to take hours to mess with the software each time that I tried to get it to work. My schedule kept me so busy that I was unable to call their customer service center during their business hours. So fixing the problem kept getting delayed. After a month, I was finally able to get through to the customer service center. The employee who "helped" me gave me instructions to "download instructions" on how to get the virus software to upgrade regularly. He said the instructions would answer all my questions. I surely hoped so, as the human version certainly wasn't going to answer them.

He was wrong. The downloaded instructions did not answer all my questions. After another month, I called once again. The changes did not fix the problem. Another month went by and I called customer service again. This time, I asked for my money back. I know the person helping me was human, but she sounded like a computer. Oh, she had a human enough voice, but each request for help to get my money back resulted in the exact same phrase *"we don't give money back."*

". . . But there must be a way."

"We don't give money back."

"I can't get this software to work"

"We don't give money back."

"I paid for software that I can't use."

"We don't give money back."

"It sounds as if you are unable to help me; please let me speak to a supervisor."

"We don't give money back."

"How about if we let the supervisor decide?"

"We don't give money back."

"Let me talk with a supervisor, and we'll let him or her decide."

"They're not going to give you your money back either."

Believe it or not, the exchange went on longer than that. The longer she went without hearing me, the harder I had to work at containing my anger. It felt like a game and that I was being mocked. My impression of the company had permanently been altered.

Customers need to be heard and have their concerns validated. Someone once said to me that hearing was mechanical and listening was mental. To truly engage listening, we must stop judging the customer and/or the customer's situation and instead, engage the brain's problem-solving power and natural curiosity. By not shutting down the judging process, we often instead shut down listening. Our brain gets caught up analyzing whether the customer is right or wrong, good or bad, fair or unfair, nice or mean, reasonable or unreasonable, liked or disliked. We must suspend that judgment process and just listen. Really listen and empathize with what the customer is saying. We must ask questions to understand the situation from their perspective. When you say, "I understand exactly how you feel," you need to *feel* it . . . you need to *mean* it.

Assumptions

Whenever I think of the word "assumptions" I am reminded of the 1970's movie *The Bad News Bears*. There was a great scene in which the coaches diagramed on a flip chart why one should never assume anything. Because when we do we make an "ass" out of "u" and "me" — Ass/u/me. As a teen, I giggled over the language being used. Bad language or not, I've never forgotten the lesson about assumptions. Yet we make them every day and get ourselves into trouble accordingly. The result leaves customers (and us) embarrassed, frustrated, and sometimes angry.

A common assumption relates to the level of a customer's knowledge. Too often, people assume customers know more than they really do. To name a few: Doctors assume patients know how to report health concerns or how to take care of themselves once given a course of treatment. Real estate agents assume customers know how the purchase process works. Airlines assume customers know how ticketing, check-in, and baggage check operates. Banks assume customers know all the services available and how to best take advantage of them.

We can easily avoid assumptions by asking open-ended questions. By taking the time to be patient and find out what a customer knows, we can then avoid assumptions and fill in the gaps in the customer's knowledge.

Another common assumption I see organizations make is with something simple — signage. I've run into these obstacles: 1) the signage is incorrect, 2) the signage is incomplete, 3) people can't easily locate the signage. Road signs are notorious for this. In recent years, I have traveled between 175 and 200 days a year. So I spend a lot of time in unfamiliar cities. I keep a great map with me, but I also rely on road signs to get me around. Many a day I've started following signs only to have the signs stop appearing. No further signs appear to indicate where I should turn next. Or, I pass the sign because it is behind a bush, faded, or so close to the turn I need to make that I'd cause an accident if I were to try. I wonder how much a city could reduce its accident rate if it improved the accuracy and condition of its signs.

As a frequent traveler, I'm at the mercy of a hotel to place correct signage. One hotel stay had me running in circles . . . literally. I took the elevator up to my floor and looked for the sign to get to my room. Strangely enough, the hotel had put the sign on the same wall as the elevator. At least I found it. I followed it left around the corner . . . then around another corner . . . then around another corner (those of you with a sense of direction have already figured out where I was headed). I ended up "around the corner" from where I started. My room was around the "right" corner from the elevator, not the left. The sign had been placed on the opposite wall from where it should have been. It gave a whole new meaning to the term "being given the run-around."

My all-time favorite signage blunder is at a restaurant in Kansas City, Missouri. As you pull into the parking lot, there is a sign pointing to the restaurant's drive-thru. However, if you follow the sign, it leads you right into a dumpster. The arrow is pointing in the opposite direction of the restaurant's drive-thru.

Signage assumptions can be easily overcome. Hire a temp for the day and give him one assignment "Find your way around the building just by using our signs." I recommend you give him a two-way radio . . . you may have to go find him.

Inconvenience/Treating the Customer as a Nuisance

It is easy for businesses to lose track of the importance of serving the customer. Too often people get caught up in serving the "business system" rather than serving the customer. Accommodating a customer doesn't mean we have to cater to the customer's every whim regardless of expense. What it does mean is that we show with our actions that we know that it is the customer who keeps our business alive. The customer is not an obstacle to getting our job done. The customer is not an interruption to our job. The customer is not an annoying part of our job. *The customer is our job.*

It seems that some businesses forget that the customer is their job. I recently moved to Kansas City. One of the first things that I had to do was get my utilities set up, including the phone service for both my home and my office. I expected to be able to arrange everything I needed with one phone call, but I wasn't able to have my order handled by one person. I had to make one phone call for the personal line and a second call for the business line, even though they were both being installed in the same house. The result was that there would be two orders and the company would try to send only one technician but couldn't make any promises. The potential was that I would be charged for two technicians, adding to my cost of the installation. No one at the phone company seemed to understand how "anti" service this was.

Fortunately for me, the end result was that one technician arrived to handle both orders. But it only drove the point further home. If one technician was qualified to handle both installations and that's the hard part of the order, why couldn't one service rep handle both orders over the phone?

Maybe it was tougher than I thought. The technician was unable to complete the work necessary because he couldn't climb the local pole that held my line. The pole was in the backyard of a neighbor who had a dog, and he was unable to determine if the dog was friendly or not. I couldn't help but think that if he stepped into the yard, he'd figure it out very quickly. It seems he hadn't tried that option. Instead, he told me I would have to ask the neighbor to put her dog inside for the day so the phone company could finish the job. He left me with instructions to call, once I'd arranged for the dog to be indoors.

Somehow, I didn't think it was my job to bother the neighbor. Neighbors can be sensitive about their pets. What a way to make a first impression: "Hi, my name is Marian. I'm your new neighbor. I want you to keep your dog inside all day so the telephone company can climb the pole in your yard." Of course, the phone company is very specific about what time they'll be by . . . "sometime between 9 and 5." You know, I just didn't see it going over very well.

Another technician was ultimately sent out. I told him the story of the other technician asking me to talk to the neighbors about their dog. He laughed and said, "Man, that guy is lazy; he'll get out of any work he can." He hit the nail on the head. The other technician was lazy. The person didn't want to do the work necessary to do the job right. In the process, I was inconvenienced.

Another area of customer inconvenience is "business hours." A business is created to make money for the owners, but it can only be done if the customers keep coming back. Businesses' services should be available when customers need them. As a previous banker, I was never able to understand the old "banker's hours" standard. Branches would close down at two in the afternoon, when the customers were still at their offices until five in the evening and unable to use our services. The two o'clock deadline served to benefit only commercial deposit accounts.

It's easy to forget that internal customers can be inconvenienced as well. Recently, I did a program for an organization that shared a difficult situation with me. It appears that employees in the Human Resource Department were having trouble getting their work done. As a team, they decided the best way to handle the situation was to close the department at two p.m. every day for "quiet time." With this new procedure, they could certainly get more work done.

What they got was *more* work. Their actions provoked hostility from every department that needed their services. The message sent was that "our needs are more important than yours." This Human Resources Department had forgotten that their co-workers were not an interruption to their work — they *were* their work.

Taking the time to make it convenient for customers to use your business is taking the high road. It is taking the time. It is changing the procedures. It is spending a little extra money. These are the ways that people form an emotional connection to you. That connection builds loyalty. A loyal customer is the lifeblood of a business.

Not Knowing Your Customer

Not long ago, I acquired a new client, a high-profile, nationally recognized, multi-billion-dollar company. I submitted a bid for four speaking engagements and was awarded two of the four. The other two were awarded to another speaker who was specifically requested by some of the audience members. In addition to the special request, the other speaker already had a proven track record with the company. The client considered me a big risk as an "unknown" speaker. It was disappointing, but I understood the necessity that I prove myself first.

The topic for the speech was customer service. Both of us would be speaking on "Knowing Your Customer to Increase Sales Opportunities."

It was my first nationally recognized client, so I was unusually nervous. It was important for me to do a great job so the company would be glad about taking a risk on me. When it came time to do the program, my nervousness escalated. I knew the client's program actually started a day before I would be speaking, so I went a day early and attended the reception and trade show. It was one of the best things I have ever done. The vendors had lots of information to share on how the company's different locations used their services. This gave me a list of ideas to share with the audience. The next day, I did the speech. It was the best performance of my career up to that time.

A few weeks later, I made the second speech and it was just as successful. In a casual conversation, I asked the client how the other speaker's programs had gone. They were "a disaster." I couldn't hide my shock and asked, "Why?" The client said, "The other speaker should have done his homework. He used a PowerPoint presentation, and, judging from the graphic effects, he put a lot of time into it, but not enough time. He used one image again and again — it was of our competitor. We were just purchased by another company; he should have used an image of our new parent company." Everyone saw the faux pas. Everyone involved was embarrassed. The speaker had been instructed to deliver a program about knowing your customer. He needed to listen to his own message.

Forgetting that Anyone is a Potential Customer

There are a few customer service stories that I never tire of telling because the message is so powerful. One such story is a situation that happened to a friend of mine. Gary worked at a car wash/gas station. He was the manager and made a good salary. But he kept himself in the money with all of his side businesses. He was always up to some new way to make an extra dollar.

He saved up for months to buy his dream car, a BMW. At 30 years old, he'd finally saved all the money he needed to buy the car. One day after work, he drove to the bank and then to the car dealership. This was a big day for him, and he was excited about it.

He walked into the car dealership and was surprised the sales staff didn't bombard him, as typically occurs. In fact, he had a bit of trouble getting their attention. Finally, one of them walked over and looked him up and down, taking special notice of his gas station uniform and the paper bag in his hand. Quietly and sternly the sales rep said, "The parts department is in the rear of the building; don't *ever* use the customer entrance again."

Without saying a word, my friend walked out the door. He was hurt, angry, and still carrying his paper bag. The bag was filled with cash, the exact amount of cash to buy the car. The dealership had forgotten that anyone could be a potential customer.

I'd like to say that this type of snootiness is of a bygone era, but it still happens daily. Ask a female friend of yours what her experience is when she walks into an upscale department store to buy high-end cosmetics, but isn't looking so upscale herself that day.

Keep in mind that just because someone is doing business with the competition now, or is not buying today, it doesn't mean the person couldn't be a buyer in the future. Anyone could be a customer. Treat each person as though he or she already is a customer, and you'll see him or her return.

Arguing with Customers

One of my favorite treats while traveling is to let someone else handle my luggage while I check into a hotel. I always point out which bag contains my computer so they can be extra careful with it. One particular business trip I was even more eager than usual to have someone help me with my bags. I was exhausted. I was staying at an old-fashioned motel in the south. It was charming, but there were no elevators and my room was on the second floor. The bell person was a welcome sight.

All of my luggage was on wheels, so it was pretty easy for him to roll it to my room. All he had to manage was the stairs. I asked him to break the luggage down and carry it up the stairs. Instead, he dragged it up the stairs like a sack of trash, with the luggage bouncing against each stair. I repeated my request, and the employee snapped back at me saying "I can handle it!" as he continued dragging the luggage, banging against each step.

When we got to my room, I asked him to break down the luggage (once again) and set the top piece on the floor. Indignantly, he said, "It'll be fine." He walked out the door, leaving my luggage just out of reach as it fell to the floor. My computer screen was shattered from the impact of the fall. My laptop is the only computer I own. The shattered screen cost me over $6000 in business because of the emails I missed while my computer was out of commission.

Oh, I was angry with myself for not arguing further with the employee. But then I realized the outrageousness of my experience as a customer. Why should I have to *argue* to get my point across? The fact is that I shouldn't have to. No customer should have to argue to receive accommodations for reasonable requests. We just want reasonable customer service.

Inefficiency

I am amazed at the inefficient service that so many businesses get away with offering their customers. Computer companies and computer stores are at the top of my list for inefficient service. I don't think any other business could get away with sending you home with a new piece of equipment that has a manual containing only about one percent of the instructions necessary to use the product. If you want more instructions, you have to go out and buy them.

This is the proverbial "rest of the story."

As soon as I returned from the trip where my computer screen was shattered, I called the store where I bought the laptop to place an order for a new screen. The service technician said he'd "have to take a look at it." I told him, "Trust me, I can identify a shattered screen." He replied that he couldn't just order a new screen for me; he'd have to see the computer "to diagnose the problem."

So between the lines, he's implying I'm an idiot, that I can't tell a shattered computer screen by looking at it and seeing the broken glass pattern in the plasma. The technician was adamant that he had to see it first. Exasperated, I relented. "When can I bring it in?" I asked.

"I've got an opening in four weeks."

He said it. He really said four weeks. He said it without embarrassment. He said it without conscience. He said it without any regard for just how poor that type of service would be.

Four weeks to look at the computer and then another two-four weeks to replace the screen "if that was the problem."

What really burned me is that I paid extra for this atrocious service. The sales clerk convinced me of how great the service would be: "We service the warranties right here in the store, whereas all the other computer stores send their computers away to be serviced." Well, maybe the other computer stores' service is better that way. Maybe they actually believe their customers when they say their computer screen is shattered. Maybe they get it repaired in a reasonable time, too, so that customers don't lose business. And maybe the other business offers a loaner while the computer is being repaired. And just maybe those other businesses are more efficient.

Lack of Integrity

It may seem like a little thing — Integrity. For some reason, we don't think about the value of "our word." We make statements, sometimes under pressure, based on what we think we should say and what we think people want to hear. We may have reasonable obstacles that prevent us from delivering on what we promise. The more valid the reason, the more we think we are justified in breaking our word. But a word broken is a word broken. And once broken, integrity suffers.

A few weeks ago, I valet parked my rental car at a downtown hotel. The valet ticket said to allow 20 minutes for the valet to return with the car. When it was time to leave, I called the valet, giving the 20-minute notice, but was pleasantly surprised to hear the valet say it would be only 10 minutes to get my car. Thirty minutes later my car was ready. What was sad was that the valet didn't understand what was wrong with the situation: "the notice says 20 minutes but I'm the only one working tonight." That's a reasonable excuse, but he'd given *his word* and now he'd broken *his word*. No matter how reasonable the excuse, his integrity has suffered.

Co-workers who depend on each other, supervisors that make promises to employees, people who assure customers that they'll "call them back" in an hour, a day, a week. It doesn't matter what type of promise. It's the promise that matters. We need to think about the promises we make and make sure that we keep them. And if for any reason we think we could fall through on the promise, we need to accommodate that in the beginning, not by saying "I'll try," but by making a more reasonable promise, one that we can be sure to keep.

Providing Incorrect or Inaccurate Information

We have become so afraid to say the words "I don't know" that people are willing to provide incorrect information in order to solve a problem. As a result, the problem usually gets worse.

Many years ago, I experienced the worst financial period of my life. On a Friday afternoon, I went through with one of the toughest decisions of my life. I left my husband. It was tough enough to deal with the situation emotionally. Financially, I was on shaky ground at best. My only credit card was "maxed out." I had to borrow money to pay the down payment and first month's rent on my apartment. It was the worst financial situation I could be in . . . until six days later. That Thursday afternoon, my boss walked into my office and laid me off. I was given only two weeks' severance.

It was two weeks before Thanksgiving. Anyone who has experienced a layoff at that time of year knows that you can consider yourself unemployed until after the New Year holidays. I knew that would be especially true for me as I held no college degree. Though I had years of experience, most people wouldn't even take the time to interview me.

I got down to my last $5 before getting a job and rebuilding my life. Though very late, and severely under minimum payment requirements, I continued to pay on my bills. As a former banker, I knew my credit was in bad shape. But I knew I could turn it around. First, I needed to find out what the credit companies required me to do, so I called every one of them. Each of the companies was helpful and gave me detailed instructions on how to get my accounts up to date.

One of the companies provided me with incorrect information. I followed the instructions the employee gave me, but he'd given me the wrong instructions. The next month my account was charged-off, destroying my credit rating for the next seven years.

I went up every level of the chain of command to vice president. None of them would take responsibility for the employee's error. I got a contrite apology and was left to deal with the consequences on my own. I was unable to rent a nice apartment and I was unable to buy a new car. This last one hurt the most. My car died just weeks after my layoff. For months I stared at the dead car until I could save the cash to buy a beater.

I've never forgotten that an employee gave me incorrect information and hurt me in the process. The company has courted me several times over the years to accept their "pre-approved card." To this day, I will not give them my business.

When we give customers inaccurate information, trust is violated. The customer has no way of knowing whether or not she will get accurate information in the future. We need to be sure we are knowledgeable in our jobs and able to admit and correct any mistakes we make along the way. Make it easy for the customer to come back.

Proving One's Self Right

The first few months that I dated my sweetheart, he sent me a dozen roses every ten days. Once he convinced me what a great guy he was, he still kept the roses coming about once a month. Each bouquet was more beautiful than the last. I was absolutely spoiled.

One afternoon, I returned from a business trip and pulled into my driveway. There, resting in a vase on my patio table was a dozen sunshine-yellow roses. Yellow is my favorite color, so I was especially excited. I took care of getting the roses inside the house before I even took my luggage out of the car.

I finished my unpacking and going through my week's mail. About an hour had passed. I went into my kitchen to enjoy my roses and found each and every one of them had wilted. They were the saddest looking buds I'd ever seen. I didn't think flowers could die so quickly.

The roses had a 24-hour guarantee, so I called the florist to let him know what had happened. The florist challenged me because the roses had been left outside. My reminder that the delivery person had left them outside didn't have any impact. The florist said the purchaser requested the roses be left outside for me if I wasn't home. He didn't think it was his responsibility to tell the purchaser that leaving them outside would likely kill the roses. He also didn't think it was his responsibility to replace the roses. Ultimately, he refused one last time and hung up on me.

The florist was determined to prove himself right. And in the process, he was willing to give up dozens of orders for roses in the future to avoid replacing the dozen that had wilted.

I still get my roses once a month and I am still spoiled. But my sweetheart makes his purchases from another place now. How about your customers? How many of them have moved on because it was more important for someone to be "right"?

Getting Even

I've read horror stories about employees getting even with customers. Each of us has heard the infamous "legends" about restaurant personnel getting even because they didn't like that the customer sent their food back.

I'd like to think that these are truly legends, but there are forms of getting even that take place every day. They are insidious. They create a negative environment. They destroy both customer and employee relationships.

We are "getting even" when we purposefully take "our own sweet time" to respond to phone calls and requests. We are getting even when we provide only the absolute minimum service required when we know someone needs more, and we get even when we purposefully let customers believe they will get their request met when we know that it will not happen. We are getting even when we could do more for a customer but choose not to.

We are getting even when we make snide remarks either to a person's face or behind his back. Co-workers of mine were witness to this when we were on a business trip. Our luggage didn't arrive at our destination city. I wasn't too worried about it; I knew it would arrive on the next flight. I wish my co-workers had been as laid back about it as I was. One of them got particularly uptight and was a bit indignant with the staff. The other co-worker asked if I could make it if my luggage didn't arrive. I said it didn't thrill me, as "all my make-up is inside my luggage, and I prefer to avoid giving my speeches *au naturel.*"

It seems one of the baggage agents found that amusing and within ear-shot of my co-worker made the comment "tell her not to wash her face tonight; she's got enough make-up on already!" The snide remark couldn't be missed. She was getting even with us because she didn't like that we were upset that our luggage didn't arrive as expected.

Customers are not always going to behave admirably. But that does not give us license to give up our principles for how we treat people. When we change our principles because we don't like what someone else is doing, we become *situationally principled.* It is hard to take the high road, but it is worth it in the end. You can respect yourself and know you did the right thing regardless of what the other person has done.

Threats/Accusations

Sometimes, folks let their anger get the best of them. I'd like to think people would know this is no way to conduct business, but the advent of email has made threats and accusations much easier.

A situation I experienced encompassed this Deadly Sin of Customer Service as well as a few others: assumptions, treating the customer as a nuisance, proving one's self right, and getting even.

The situation was innocuous enough as I was house hunting in a new city. I contacted a real estate agent whose name I'd seen on a for sale sign. She was pleasant enough, so I asked for her help in finding my first home. She signed me up for an on-line service and that was the end of it. She didn't help me with neighborhoods, or financing, or identifying potential houses. It was up to me to find a house using the on-line service.

I flew into town and asked to see a couple of houses I'd found. The agent's lack of interest was evident and it was beginning to annoy me. After all, wouldn't she make a good commission off my purchase?

I had only one more day in town, so a friend and I decided to drive by one of the houses again. I'd called the agent to show the house to us again, but she wasn't returning my calls. When looking for the house, my friend made a wrong turn. We ended up in front of this gorgeous house with a sale sign in front of it. A bunch of folks were in the front yard, so we asked if they had any flyers they could give us on the house. They didn't have a flyer; instead, they offered to let us go through the house right then. The people in the yard were the owners with their real estate agent, Judy.

The house was perfect, and Judy was undeniably helpful. The original agent finally called back after ten that evening. I told her I no longer needed to see the original house again. I'd changed my mind about it.

When I called Judy the next morning, I not only told her I wanted to put a contract on the new house, I asked her to be my agent. I was dissatisfied with the other agent. Judy wanted to check with her broker first. After looking into it, Judy and her broker discovered the other agent never had me sign an agreement to be represented by her. So they decided it was fine for me to switch agents. Out of professional courtesy, Judy contacted the other agent to let her know what had happened.

What then transpired shocked me. I received an email from the other agent that was dripping with nasty sarcasm. It was titled, "congratulations Marian!!!!!!!!!!!!!!!!!!!!!!!!!" As if the multitude of exclamation points were necessary. In her email, she claimed she had spent dozens of hours helping me, she accused me of lying about my changing my mind about the first home that I'd seen, and ultimately stated that my kind of person would be dishonest with my clients as well. I knew the truth, but once an accusation is made, a shadow of doubt is created. This woman was threatening my livelihood.

I was already under great stress from buying my first home. Now I had someone implying that my business would be negatively affected (she was personal friends with the owner of a business that was my largest client). This woman was actually threatening me over a perceived slight and attempting to get even.

I was afraid I had no control over the situation, but ultimately the respective brokers of the two agents got involved. My situation is now a case study for broker training meetings on what *not* to do with clients.

I have no doubt that the other agent thinks I purposefully tried to hurt her. My only intention was to find myself a house in a short time period. I had to find someone who could help me do that. Threatening me only served to verify she was not the agent to help me find my first home.

So there you have the Deadly Dozen: Refusing to listen, acknowledge, or validate; Assumptions; Inconvenience/Treating the Customer as a Nuisance; Not Knowing Your Customer; Forgetting that Anyone is a Potential Customer; Arguing with Customers; Inefficiency; Lack of Integrity; Providing Incorrect or Inaccurate Information; Proving One's Self Right; Getting Even; and Threats/Accusations. Having an effective customer service program is important to every business. A critical part of that program is teaching employees to avoid the Deadly Dozen. It's easy to take the low road when we are tired, frustrated, overworked, and feeling abused by customer or employer. Taking the high road means avoiding the Deadly Dozen. It requires being self-aware. It requires being vigilant. It requires effective coaching and support from management. Violating the Deadly Dozen hurts our businesses financially and hurts our morale internally. What will your commitment be to rid your organization of the Deadly Dozen?

ABOUT MARIAN MADONIA

Marian Madonia is a professional speaker, author, and trainer. She helps audiences embrace change, communicate more effectively, deliver great customer service, and deal with difficult and "attitudinally challenged" people. Her style is straight-up, down-to-earth and funny. Marian began speaking professionally over 15 years ago for corporations and industry associations. In 1997, she began Madonia Communications Int'l, dedicated to the principle, "Live, laugh, learn, and never give up!" Her clients range from priests to prisoners as her diverse clientele includes The Archdiocese of Detroit, Mail Boxes Etc., Assante Canada, and the State of Indiana. She is a Professional member of the National Speakers Association, a past officer of National Speakers Association Tennessee, and a graduate of Georgetown University's Training Specialist program. Her audiences know her best for her humor and her honesty.

Contact Information:
Marian Madonia
Madonia Communications Int'l
4741 Central Street, #115
Kansas City, MO 64112
Phone: (816) 237-8700
E-mail: Marian@MarianMotivates.com
Website: www.MarianMotivates.com

GOING THE EXTRA MILE TO BUILD LOYALTY AND BOOST YOUR PROFITS

by Debra J. Schmidt, M.S.

"The number one loyalty killer is the difference between a customer's expectations and his or her actual experience."
— Debra J. Schmidt

Fine Customer Service, or . . .
I'll See You Until I Find Someone Better

Have you ever had a terrible customer service experience at a restaurant? When you were leaving, did the host or hostess ask, "How was everything?" Instead of offering your real opinion, did you simply answer, "FINE"?

Most of us leave it at "fine" for a number of reasons. We don't want to waste our time trying to fix their business; we don't believe anyone will listen to our concerns; and even if they do listen, we don't believe anything will change. So we say "fine" and walk out the door vowing never to return. Then, on Monday morning, we go to work and tell everyone how awful our experience was at that restaurant.

"FINE" is the most dangerous word in the consumer language. It's a code word that means, "I'm neutral — and as soon as I find something better, I'm out of here!"

Are your customers telling you that everything is fine, implying they are satisfied? If so, you may have a problem — because 65-85 percent of customers who say they are satisfied actually *switch* to the competition. Customers will not continue to do business with us for long if we simply meet their expectations. In order to build loyalty within them, we must exceed their expectations by looking for ways to surprise and delight them.

Don't settle for your customers or employees checking the "satisfied" box on your satisfaction surveys. Instead, find ways to surprise and delight them by exceeding their expectations. Then they will be writing on your survey comment lines: "The employees here are always friendly." "This company goes the extra mile for me." "The employees sincerely care about my concerns."

When you begin receiving this type of feedback from your customers, you'll know you're on your way to building loyalty.

Loyalty Starts at the Top

Today's businesses are losing customers and employees in record numbers. Customer loyalty is on the decline, but many companies are treating the symptoms instead of the causes of their customer retention problems.

Set your goals to create loyal customers. But keep in mind that customer loyalty starts with the internal customers — employees and co-workers; and it's a top-down initiative. It must start with the CEO or business owner. In order to build loyalty, we need to find ways to surprise and delight our employees and customers to exceed their expectations.

Consider the following:

- If you're losing employees, you're losing customers. On average, American companies lose half of their employees every four years and half of their customers every five years. This suggests that employee attrition may have a significant impact on customer loyalty.

- Employee attitudes are significantly affected by the way employees are treated by upper management. One of the most important aspects of improving customer retention is a total commitment to loyalty by the CEO or business owner. This commitment must be demonstrated daily at all levels of the organization for the employees to clearly observe.

- Customer loyalty is the responsibility of everyone within an organization. In order to create a loyalty-focused culture, customer service training needs to start at the top.

- CEOs, business owners, and senior management also need to recognize that their employees are their primary customers. Employees deserve and expect the same caring service that is given to the external customers.

- Customer loyalty is earned by consistently exceeding customer and employee expectations with outstanding service. This level of service can be achieved only when managers are held accountable for their internal customer service skills: in other words, for how they deal with their employees and co-workers.

To create both loyal customers and employees, focus on building long-term relationships with each one on an individual basis. Take time to listen to them. Greet them warmly when they call, and use their name at least three times in every conversation. Thank your customers and employees frequently, and find ways to show them how much they are valued.

When you focus on building loyalty, both employee and customer retention go up. The end result — a boost in your profits!

Calculating the Lifetime Value of Your Customers

When you lose a single customer, you do not lose one sale, but a lifetime opportunity of profitability with that individual. Do you know the average lifetime value of your customers?

To determine the average lifetime value of your customers, estimate how much they will spend with your business on a monthly or annual basis, and multiply it by the number of years they could potentially use your products or services. For example, if an average grocery customer purchases $100 worth of grocery products per week, 52 weeks a year, for approximately 45 years — that customer's average lifetime value will be $234,000.

Oops. Don't stop there. Next, factor in how much your customers could potentially increase their spending each year because they're thrilled with your products or services. There's more! Now start calculating the value of all of the new customers that your loyal customers will refer to your business.

Here are some examples of the average lifetime values of customers in a variety of industries:

Life insurance owner	$87K
Automobile owner	$200K
Grocery customer	$234K+
Medical patient	$1 million+

Increasing customer retention by as little as 5 percent can translate into as much as a 100 percent increase in profitability. It is important for all employees within an organization to understand the lifetime value of customers. Then they can focus on building relationships with the very people who keep you in business.

The Cost of Replacing Customers

It costs five to six times more to attract new customers than to keep old ones, and it costs sixteen times more to get a new customer to the same level of profitability as a loyal customer. Customer loyalty and the lifetime value of a customer can be worth up to ten times as much as the price of a single purchase.

Richard F. Gerson, the author of *Beyond Customer Service: Keeping Customers For Life*, says, "Businesses that provide superior customer service can charge more, realize greater profits, increase their market share and have customers willingly pay more for their products simply because of good service. In fact, you can gain an average of 6 percent a year in market share simply by providing good service: satisfying and keeping your customers."

The lifetime value of a customer is worth providing refunds when a customer returns a purchase. Such a policy generates good will, and positive word of mouth and builds loyalty. Customer service is governed by the rule of 10's. If it costs $10,000 to get a new customer, it takes only ten seconds to lose one, and ten years for the customer to get over it.

Poor service is expensive, but good customer service is invaluable. Customer retention directly affects the bottom line, and it can be accomplished only through a focused customer retention program.

Defining Customer Service

As implied by the phrase, customer service involves serving the customer. However, there is bad customer service, which drives the customer away; "fine" customer service, which meets the bare minimum of service criteria, but puts your business at risk; and then there is *going the extra mile,* with all the bells and whistles.

How to Get from "Bad" to "Great!" Customer Service

Careful observation of employee behaviors will help you identify the service sins being committed in your company. But simply pointing out these problem behaviors won't get you very far toward improving them — you need to provide concrete improvement tactics, and you need to make all employees part of the solution, not single them out as the cause of the problem.

Once it gets going, your employee team will probably come up with some terrific ways to improve your customer service. To get them started, however, consider the following tips:

- Make your customer's problem your problem.
- Seek regular, direct contact with customers to build strong relationships.

- Anticipate their needs and develop a reputation for responsiveness.

- If your customer is upset or has a problem, take care of it as soon as possible and follow up to make sure it's resolved. Don't rely on someone else to do it.

- Treat each customer as you would want to be treated.

- Show complete understanding for each customer's concerns, even if you don't agree with the person.

- It is not our job to "teach our customers a lesson" when they have made an error. Simply provide the service they need and refrain from scolding them.

- Remember your customers' birthdays, children's names, and any special needs.

- SMILE.

- Be an encouragement to your customers. Yours may be the only kind word they hear today.

- Remove service obstacles even if it means bending the rules at times.

- Show respect for your customers and their schedules by being on time.

- If you are already meeting customer expectations — list three things you can do to *exceed* their expectations!

- Introduce your support staff to your customers. People in support roles at many companies often spend their entire careers without meeting any customers face to face. Remedy this situation by bringing a support staff member on a sales call. The cost of the trip is nothing next to the motivation it will bring. The support staff will get a better feel for customers and will appreciate the fact that you value them enough to introduce them to important clients.

- And finally, provide the best customer service at a competitive market price.

What Does It Mean to "Go the Extra Mile"?

Customer expectations are so low these days that it is really quite simple to meet them. When you meet your customers' expectations, they will be satisfied and hopefully will continue to do business with you. I say "hopefully" because satisfied customers are neutral and often leave if they find better service elsewhere.

In order to move your customers from the status of "satisfied" to the profitable status of "loyal," it is essential to exceed their expectations. This process occurs through value-added service or "going the extra mile."

Think of value added service as a baker's dozen; you promise twelve donuts, but deliver thirteen. In other words, you surprise your customers with service they didn't expect.

Some examples of value-added service include:

- Free button and hem repair offered by a drycleaner.
- A "thank you" note with a coupon for a discount on the next visit.
- A long-stemmed red rose placed on the "birthday girl's" table by a restaurant manager.
- A washed and vacuumed car after an automotive service has been performed.

The list goes on. But when you can delight your customers with unexpected service, it is value-added. In other words, when you deliver more than was promised, customer loyalty increases. Get together with your staff and hold a breakfast brainstorming session on all the ways you can build value-added activities into your business.

Target Your Extra Mile Efforts

Delivering value-added service is only one way to exceed your customers' expectations. You can set high standards when providing all aspects of customer service.

Give focus to your customer service efforts by setting targeted goals. For example:

1. Welcoming Customers

2. Valuing Customers

3. Thanking Customers

4. Going The Extra Mile

Welcoming Customers:

- Welcome them to your company.

- Follow the 10-10 Rule (Greet customers within 10 seconds of coming within 10 feet of them).

- Smile and make eye contact.

- Make sure all voice-mail messages are warm, friendly, and welcoming.

- Invite them back.

Valuing Customers:

- Remove service obstacles whenever possible.

- Tell them how they can take advantage of special offers.

- Let them know how long telephone wait times may be.

- Use their name if known. If he or she is a regular customer, ask for a name.

- Patiently answer their questions.

- Take time with each customer. Don't rush service or let your tone of voice imply that you're too busy to help.

Thanking Customers:

- Thank the customer who expresses a complaint, and take action to get it resolved.
- Thank a customer for trying out a new service or product.
- Thank a customer for patience if waiting was necessary.

Extra Mile Service:

- Offer to follow up with additional information.
- Point out other services you've provided.
- Ask how their experience was and if they have suggestions for improvements.
- Refer them to the competition if your own company does not offer what they need.
- Listen carefully to their needs and offer creative suggestions.

Take Notes from My Orthodontist

When I think of great customer service, I think of my orthodontist, Dr. Randall Moles. During every visit, I observe Dr. Moles and his employees "going the extra mile" for their patients. Here are just a few of the things you can count on when you visit Moles Orthodontics in Milwaukee, Wisconsin:

- A warm welcome accompanied by a big smile and a personal greeting (they actually remember your name).
- A wait time of usually ten minutes or less.
- Lots of things to do while you are waiting (fresh coffee, current magazines, children's books and electronic Gameboys,™ to name a few).
- A free T-shirt for all new patients.
- Complete accountability and a sincere apology if a scheduling problem occurs.

- Invitations to customer appreciation "movie days" sponsored by the clinic. Our whole family was invited to a free movie at a local theater along with other patients.

- Follow-up phone calls to educate you about the next steps in your dental process.

- Sincere respect and appreciation by employees, not only for the patients but also for their co-workers.

Now, it is true that Dr. Moles is an outstanding orthodontist. But I'm convinced that the reason his practice is so successful is that he and his entire staff consistently deliver service that exceeds the expectations of his patients. This orthodontist gave a whole new meaning to the phrase "service with a smile!"

Prescription for Success

I was certain I had stepped back in time to the 1950's when I walked into Dan Fitzgerald Pharmacy in Whitefish Bay, Wisconsin. The store is modern and has all the latest supplies, but it was the personalized service that caught me off-guard.

As I walked up to the prescription counter, the pharmacist stepped out, took an elderly lady by the arm, and gently led her to another area of the store. On his way to showing her where the cold medicine was located, he stopped, smiled and apologized to me for not being at the prescription counter but promised he'd be right back.

Before I could close my mouth, which was agape with astonishment, the checkout clerk greeted me with a smile and apologized again for the delay in service. The pharmacist was gone all of four minutes!

When he returned, he came directly over to me to get my prescription information and hurried behind the counter to get my refill. It was ready in a matter of minutes. He stepped back out to hand it to me and said, "I suggest the alligator measuring spoon; it'll make it more fun for your son to take his medicine."

As I paid for the prescription, the clerk thanked me for coming in and complimented me on the earrings I was wearing. When I left, three people waved goodbye! If I weren't sitting at my desk as I write this, I'd swear I was in Mayberry. I'm thinking of starting a customer service training program called, "Learning to Be Like Aunt Bea!"

Special Delivery

Late one night I was completing my final preparations for two seminars I was scheduled to deliver the following day. When I inspected the workbooks, I discovered that several of them had been assembled incorrectly. I was in a panic. Here it was 8 p.m. and I was due to begin my programs the next morning at 8 a.m.

Insty-Prints was already closed, but, fortunately, I remembered the last name of one of the employees. I located her name in the phonebook and called her at home. Although the error had taken place at the binding company, not at the printer, this employee took complete ownership of the problem. She apologized for the inconvenience, drove to our home to pick up the workbooks, went back to Insty-Prints, reprinted and personally bound several workbooks. She called to let me know they were completed so I could relax, and then she delivered them back to our home.

Bright and early the next morning . . . the show went on — and a perfect set of workbooks was distributed to the participants.

One employee, who took complete ownership of a problem and resolved it quickly, cemented this trainer's loyalty to Milwaukee's North Shore Insty-Prints for a long time to come

All Aboard!

When I took my six-year-old son on his first train trip to Chicago, we carefully selected our seats for the best view. He was so excited when we pulled out of the station. We were chatting about all of our plans when we heard laughter.

We looked up to see Senior Conductor Richard Misunas strolling down the aisle, welcoming everyone. He stopped to ask each passenger if anyone needed any information about Chicago.

Richard shared tips about which sights to see, the best ways to get around, and where to find maps, great restaurants and much, much more.

When he got to our seats, he greeted us with a warm smile and gave us tips on how to get to the museums using the free trolley service. My son turned to me and said, "Wow. What a nice guy."

During the rest of the trip, Richard used the intercom to point out historical sites and entertain all of us with humorous stories.

As I strolled through our train car, I saw lots of smiles, even on the faces of the harried business commuters. Thanks, Richard, for going the extra mile to make this a train trip to remember. What a wonderful example you set for my son!

More Extra Miles

People frequently ask me to give them creative ideas on how to build loyalty with their customers. Here are more examples of how businesses are "going the extra mile."

- During the holidays, an insurance agent in Milwaukee sent out two 9-volt batteries to each of his past and present clients. Included with the batteries was a handwritten note that read, "I care about you and your family. Please change the batteries in your smoke detectors."

- At a Wisconsin hotel, the staff washes the windshield of every one of its guests' automobiles each morning. The guest finds a note that reads: "We wanted to start your day off "bright." Thank you for staying with us and have a safe trip."

- A veterinarian sends out a sympathy card signed by every member of his staff when one of his clients loses a pet.

- An automotive service center assigns an employee to drive customers to work or home and to pick them up again when the repair work is completed.

Your Customers Are Your Job Security

We hear a great deal about layoffs and downsizing today. Some can't be prevented in today's economy. However, other businesses are laying off workers because their customers are going to the competition. Today, clients and customers want much better quality than before. They expect top-notch service or they'll take their business to your competitors. Not your problem? Think again!

Your job security depends on how valuable you are to your customers. The better you serve them, the better you protect your career. If we take our jobs for granted, we take our customers for granted, and that's a risky way to run a career.

Expect your employer to expect more from you. The marketplace is demanding far more these days from the organization itself. The more you allow your service to go soft, the greater the odds you could end up in some downsizing statistics.

Or, the organization might simply decide to outsource your work. More than likely, you're actually in competition with external providers who offer the same service, whether you realize it or not. In the final analysis, customers are your only source of job security.

ABOUT DEBRA J. SCHMIDT, M.S.

*D*ebra J. Schmidt, known as "the Loyalty Builder," is the owner of *Spectrum Consulting Group Inc. based in Milwaukee. She works with people who want to grow their business by building customer loyalty, boosting sales and developing effective marketing strategies. Her diverse client list includes Northwestern Mutual, Kohler Co. and the Green Bay Packers. Debra is an entrepreneur, television personality, Emmy Award nominee, and winner of six national marketing awards. She is also an in-demand business consultant and speaker. She is the author of* 101 Ways to Build Customer Loyalty. *For a free subscription to "The Loyalty Builder," Spectrum Consulting Group's electronic newsletter loaded with tips and strategies for growing your business, visit her website.*

Contact Information:
Debra Schmidt
Spectrum Consulting Group Inc.
P.O. Box 170954
Milwaukee, WI 53217-8086
Phone: (414) 964-3872
Fax: (414) 967-0875
E-mail: Deb@TheLoyaltyBuilder.com
Website: www.TheLoyaltyBuilder.com

SALES AND PROFITS: 5-1/2 WAYS TO DELIVER SUPER SERVICE INSIDE!

by Ron Rael

The Ace Hardware store located in my neighborhood is a great place to shop. Tim, the owner/manager, has raised customer service to an art form. As a direct result, the store's sales have significantly increased ever since Tim arrived. Tim's growing customer base prefers to shop there instead of the local discount super hardware store, all because he is purposely bucking the current trend of minimizing service to reduce costs.

Each time I go in there, I get a chance to see true customer service in action. These are the five things that Tim's team does so well:

✓ Fosters communication within the sales team

✓ Sells knowledge instead of products

✓ Tickles each customer's "IVY" bone

✓ Recognizes and rewards great service

✓ Measures successes

To grow your firm's sales and profits, you must be able to deliver super service inside your organization. The key to making this happen is to use these same five techniques that you use to deliver super service outside. As we all know, when you have the structure in place to create happy, satisfied, and loyal clients, your sales and profits will soar!

While most information about customer service is oriented to the outside customer or client — those who "pay the bills" — another dimension that is just as important is inside, or internal, customer service.

Principles Related to Internal Customer

1. Everyone in our organization has at least one internal customer who must be pleased.

2. The quality of service we deliver to the external customer is a direct reflection of the quality of service we give to each other inside the business.

3. Excellent outside service can exist only when it is driven by excellent inside support.

This chapter explains why these three basic principles about internal service are true and gives you a specific 5-1/2-step strategy for nurturing a culture in which delivering super service inside is the norm.

Fantastic Customer Service Starts With Your Culture

*Corporate culture is the story we enact each day
that defines who we are.*

The starting point to building a strategy for improving and maintaining super service internally is to examine your corporate culture.

What is culture and why is it important? Corporate culture is the mood, attitude, and atmosphere of an organization. It has an effect on nearly every aspect of your business. The shorthand way of explaining culture is, "How things are done around here!"

✓ How we treat one another

✓ How complaints and disagreements are handled

✓ How resources are shared

✓ How information is handled and managed

The wellspring for all this is your culture. Culture is not as nebulous as you might think; instead it is somewhat concrete. There are ten components that make up your firm's culture, and each is interrelated and interconnected to the others. Think of corporate culture as a mosaic of these ten elements.

Mosaic of Corporate Culture

Communications	Ceremonies & Events
Customs & Norms	Goals & Measurements
Leader's Attitudes, Behaviors, Beliefs	Training
Organizational Structure	Policies & Procedures
Rewards & Recognition	Physical Environment

In a mosaic, you cannot leave out one piece nor can you move one piece without affecting the rest. Each piece by itself does not make the whole; all the parts together do. Corporate culture is just like that. For example, if you attempt to raise the level of customer service by improving internal communications, there will be no lasting improvement unless the other nine elements are also improved.

Every One of Us Has a Customer — Principle 1

Everybody's gotta serve someone.

One reason it can be challenging to improve internal service is that the definition of *who my customer is* remains unclear. The employees who work with the external customer clearly know who their client is, and they have regular interactions with him/her.

Take the employee who works in accounting, entering invoices and making payments to suppliers. *Who is his customer?*

- The vendor?
- The employee who does the purchasing?
- The executive to whom he delivers a weekly status report?
- The controller who signs the checks?

The same logic about the external customer holds true for the inside customer. Every day we must justify our existence to the client who pays us money for what we provide. This is the ultimate measure of success in business. The same applies to the inside customer — to whom do I justify my purpose for the work that I do?

The Level of Service We Deliver is the Same — Principle 2

> *Outside customer service is a mirror — it reflects how well*
> *the inside customers are being satisfied and served.*

How a firm treats its external customers and clients derives from the employees' attitudes about the products or services delivered. When an employee resents the work or harbors negative feelings about the client, it shows up in everything he or she does.

The same is true for the internal customer. If I feel that you do not value the work I am performing for you, I won't care about the quality of my work. If you think that the tasks *I* am performing do not enhance the job that *you* do, then you believe that I am just pushing paper.

These attitudes about the work we perform for each other reflect in the quality of our work products, in how we communicate with one another, and in our unity or disharmony. Customers are smart! They pick up on bad attitudes and disgruntled employees. If this negativity is a regular occurrence, the customer will go buy from someone who is not so difficult to work with.

I was shopping at a department store selecting a suit for an important presentation at a national conference. The sales professional was doing all the right things, asking great questions, showing me a wide selection of options, and suggesting accessories that I had missed. All combined, the clothes I was about to buy were worth a healthy commission to him. When the tailor showed up for the fitting, I felt an immediate coolness as he entered the room. The tailor was uncommunicative, and when he did speak he was surly. The salesman disagreed with the tailor's suggestions, and the tailor barked back at the sales pro. I felt awkward being caught in the middle of this tussle. From the words being said, this sounded like a continuing feud.

Ann, my wife, who goes with me when I shop for clothing, felt so uncomfortable she got up and left. I followed. A competitor where the employees really support one another received my business that day and still does.

Excellent External Service Comes From Excellent Internal Support — Principle 3

Never build your dream castle on a hill made of sand.

Mary was shopping for a tax consultant. Her return was complicated, and the company she worked for had paid for her move to a new home, so she really wanted good advice.

Since she did not have any contacts in Seattle yet, she got a listing from the Washington Society of CPA's and started calling the ones close to her home. On her third call, she contacted a firm whose entire staff was attending a company retreat. Cindy, the teenage daughter of one of the firm partners, was answering the phone and taking messages. Cindy attended college and often did filing and clerical work when the firm had a need.

After Mary described her need, Cindy raved about her dad's firm. She told Mary a brief story about how her dad had saved a client lots of money. Then Cindy bragged about the leading-edge information system the firm used to help clients with tax planning. Mary was impressed with Cindy's enthusiasm and respect for her father's firm.

Mary became a client of that firm and within two years so did several of Mary's colleagues and even her new employer. Mary was so thrilled with her CPA that she constantly recommends the firm to other people. That rewarding relationship all started because of Cindy's helpful attitude.

Sales don't arrive magically at your door. Generating a sale and delivering the product or service demands a team approach. From the marketing group to the sales group to the customer service group and on into the shipping department, from the warehouse group to accounting and the collections department, everyone has a key role in satisfying the external customer.

Keep Our Bull's Eye On the Prize

Everyone impacts the ultimate customer.

One of the best ways to enhance your strategy of super internal service and support is to ensure that everyone in the organization sees how close he/she is to the real customer.

Whenever I coach clients on creating a culture of service, I show them this diagram. If it looks like a bull's eye, then your eyesight is perfect. The center of the bull's eye is the reason your firm exists — to satisfy this ever-changing and often fickle person we call the customer. To ensure that everyone in your company keeps an eye on the prize, the bull's eye chart shows how far removed from the true customer each employee is — one step at the most.

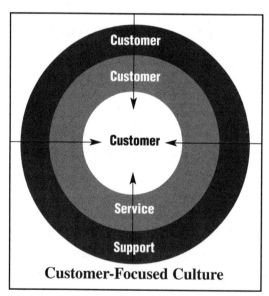

Customer Service Teams
Sales
Marketing
Customer Service
Warranty Service
Distributions
Shipping
Collections

Customer Support Teams
Accounting
Human Resources
Research & Development
Training
Executives
Administration

My clients prefer this method of viewing how a customer-driven culture works. The value of this bull's eye approach is that it visibly shows to all the internal departments that they exist to satisfy their own customers, those on the inner ring or within their own ring.

Now that I have convinced you without a doubt (no ego here) that inside customer service is just as important as external service, let's consider how to nurture a culture of super service.

Here is a 5-1/2-step strategy that will dramatically boost the level of internal customer support and improve your ability to deliver fantastic service to the external customer. Super internal support leads to fantastic external service, which leads to higher sales and profits.

Step 1 — Foster Communication

The firm that communicates well profits as well.

Tim, the owner/manager of my neighborhood Ace Hardware, equipped every employee with a headset. By wearing these instruments, the employees ensure that every customer call is answered immediately. Another benefit of this technology is that employees can communicate with one another instantaneously.

Whenever I am in the store, I see how well this works. A customer comes in asking for Tim, and immediately Tim is notified that he is "needed up front." Another customer asks the cashier for the location of a pipe, and, within seconds, the expert in plumbing is escorting that customer to the correct aisle.

Long lines at the cash register are avoided because as soon as more than three people fill a line, the cashier pushes a button and calls over a second or third cashier.

Super internal customer service has the same need for fostering communication. It is important to see internal communication as a "handoff." In the game of football the handoff is the most critical play because it constitutes over half the plays during a typical game. Disaster could result if the ball is dropped when the quarterback hands off the ball to another player. The same is true in striving for super inside service. All day long, we hand off crucial information to one another, and if the information is not handed off correctly and in a timely manner, disaster may result!

When your corporate culture is healthy, people will want to use the headset, as in Tim's hardware store. When the culture is dysfunctional, employees will undermine communication.

By employing these specific actions, you will immediately foster better communication that, in turn, builds super internal support.

✓ Use a cross-functional approach to assigning teams for all projects. Any department that has a stake in the project's outcome needs to be represented at all project meetings. This person becomes the nexus of information in and out of the project team.

✓ Attend staff meetings of the other departments that are your customers and invite them to attend yours. This practice fosters communication while raising awareness of both problems and opportunities. It also builds trust among different departments. The time invested now will pay off with time saved later.

Step 2 — Sell Knowledge Instead of Products

We are all in the information business, and we are only as good as the products we supply to our customers and clients.

Whether we sell windows, books, advertisement, tax returns, houses, or office machines, we are all in the information business. You sell information in the form that your customers or clients use to improve their lives or their businesses.

In the internal processes of all companies, every department uses its own lingo, tools, and methods. What often stymies super inside support is that we don't understand what each other does.

We need to focus on how my work products and information impact your products and information. All of your work is a link in the chain of everything the company does. So I need to know what you do and why you do it, and you need the same understanding about me.

Whenever information between departments is not shared as part of an integrated process to getting our work done, silos develop. Where silos exist, department heads fight over rather than share resources. When we spend time squabbling over who gets a bigger slice of the pie, the ultimate loser is the external customer.

A legal firm is a fast-paced business and Elsa knows this. She manages all her firm's administrative areas. While the lawyers bring in the business, her job is to support the firm's efforts to retain clients. One way she is successful in doing this is to keep her staff informed and to keep all channels of communication open.

"One hallmark of how well we do this is that in my staff of twenty, we have had almost no turnover in the twelve years I have been here." This is amazing, considering the pressures, rush deadlines, and varied personalities who work in the profitable and successful Seattle firm.

When I asked Elsa how she nurtures a culture in which the proper handoff of information is the norm, she named these strategies:

✓ She treats her employees as intelligent.

✓ She works for them.

✓ Before she delegates a task, she does it first to become familiar with what is required.

✓ She is always frank and honest.

✓ She treats her employees with respect.

✓ She reminds everyone to "communicate, communicate, communicate."

✓ She remains friendly, no matter what.

By employing these actions, you will get employees focused on the importance of sharing their most important product, knowledge.

✓ Since so much of our communication takes place via e-mail, set up a priority system to your e-mail messages. In the "re:" section, use a priority code to represent the urgency or importance of the subject. Before implementing this, take these two steps: 1) Obtain full agreement on the meaning of each level of priority and the response time required for each; and 2) Keep the system simple with no more than three levels. Complexity will kill any benefits.

✓ With your team, create a list of the information "products" you regularly provide to your customers. Design a simple chart that shows how information flows to and from your internal customers. Add to this map crucial information, such as the deadlines, sources, storage locations, and precision or quality required. Place this map in a location that is visible for your team. Update it as you obtain feedback from your various customers. (See Step 5)

Step 3 — Tickle the Customer's IVY bone

Show me that you love me, tell me that you care.

Every one of us craves to have our "IVY" bone tickled.

I
Value
You

The best companies demonstrate to their customers that "we value your business." The firms with super internal support visibly demonstrate that each department or team values the others.

Mandy took over the human resources (HR) department of a firm that was experiencing growing pains. Most employees viewed the HR function as a "necessary evil." Mandy recognized that in order for the firm's employees to change their opinions of HR, she needed her department to deliver super service.

She developed a team approach for all employees involved in the HR functions at all the widespread branches. Through a series of meetings, retreats, and one-on-one coaching, she helped each HR employee connect with the value that he or she provided others within the firm.

As a team, the HR employees created a value-oriented vision and drafted a brochure on the various services they provided internally. The final step for Mandy's team was to describe how HR supported the firm in achieving its goals and mission. Her entire team gave a presentation to every department in the company. Almost overnight, managers' attitudes toward the HR function improved. The HR team is now used as a value-adding resource. Today, nearly every one of the 400 employees sees HR as an asset to the firm.

Here are specific actions you can take to start tickling the "IVY" bones of your internal customers.

✓ Cross train outside of your department. HR employees need to spend a day a week helping out in accounting. Accounting employees need to assist warehouse employees in doing their job. Warehouse employees see what their customer's world is like when they file, answer phones, or process paperwork. This ensures that each internal employee walks in his or her client's shoes regularly.

✓ Encourage each internal support department to manage itself as its own company, complete with products (information) and customers (users of the information). Encourage the department to hold weekly staff meetings in which problems, challenges, needs, and resources are dealt with. Have every employee visit with his/her customers regularly, just as an outside sales person would.

Step 4 — Recognize and Reward Super Service

There are no I's in the word "team" . . .
but there are two in "incentives."

When Jennie showed up for her shift at Starbuck's, the mess in the refrigerator appalled her. Someone on the evening shift had spilled something in there, but because of the high volume of business, no one had the time to completely clean it up.

Even though she had other tasks to perform and customers to serve, Jennie created the time to clean the refrigerator. She thought no one had noticed and forgot about it. Her boss and other employees did take notice. The next day, Jennie was recognized with a MUG award for her super-service on the refrigerator.

Jennie said, "I felt honored. I felt good. It was a nice warm-fuzzy to be recognized for doing my job." She proudly showed me her MUG pin she received for her contribution.

The Starbuck's MUG award stands for:

> **M**oves of
> **U**ncommon
> **G**reatness

Starbuck's, one of the top-rated places to work, regularly provides fantastic service to its external customers. The partners of Starbuck's give that same high-quality service to each other. This culture of fantastic service is supported by the company's many methods of rewarding and recognizing one another. The MUG award, given to a partner who does something special, says *"we noticed and applaud you for it."*

Jennifer, who works with Jennie, has been recognized three times by her peers. She said this about her first MUG: "I was really excited about getting it. I felt really good. I was brand new and had not received any formal evaluation yet." She received her award for taking on extra cleaning duties while the experienced partners handled a huge rush of customers.

Another way Starbuck's encourages super customer service is through a formal recognition program. It is called BRAVO and is given to the partner who visibly demonstrates a commitment to the Starbuck's mission of "Growing Our Bean Stock."

Here are actions you can take to use rewards and recognition as a way to reinforce a culture of super inside support:

✓ Conduct an anonymous survey of employees for each of your formal recognition programs. Ask:
  - *What message does this reward send out to employees?*
  - *What positive behaviors arise from this recognition?*
  - *What undesirable behaviors arise from this recognition?*
  Use this information to evaluate the effectiveness of each reward.

✓ Brainstorm with each internal support manager to generate at least a half-dozen ways to give spontaneous recognition for super service internally. Be sure to vary the rewards and simplify the criteria. After launching this process, stay aware of any changes in the level of internal customer service. Revise and improve as needed.

Step 5 — Measure Your Successes

Feedback is the nourishment for super inside support.

"Feedback is the breakfast of champions." This phrase, made famous by Ken Blanchard in *The One Minute Manager*, holds true for super internal customer service, too.

Every year companies spend enormous amounts of resources to survey their external clients and customers. The best companies use this information to improve the level of service. They survey often to see if the level of service has changed.

Leaders of the internal support departments must do the same type of surveying regularly. Each customer you have needs the chance to express opinions in three specific areas.

1. How well are we serving you now?
2. What can we do to better serve you?
3. What are we not doing now that we could do to better support you?

As part of my customized process for coaching a client on creating a culture of super service, I have each internal department develop its own feedback tool, create a simple method for getting the feedback, and decide what to do with the information.

Here are six lessons I have learned to ensure that the survey provides the feedback champions need:

✓ The person responding must be able to complete the survey in less than 10 minutes — any longer and it won't get done.

✓ Visit the person responding for his/her department to explain the purpose of the survey and explain how the information will be used.

✓ Make it easy for the person to respond by a specific deadline.

✓ Thank the person responding for taking the time to give your team feedback.

✓ Keep each customer apprised of the improvements you are making as a result of the combined feedback.

✓ Survey each customer at least twice a year.

To ensure that the time you invest in this survey pays off, here are some cautions:

✗ Do not do a survey unless you will really use the information to improve.

✗ Expect negative results the first time, especially if you are not providing super service.

✗ Expect some resistance, especially if your team or service is not perceived as adding value to the customer.

✗ Whatever your feedback is the first time, it is your baseline and should only get better.

✗ Expect less than full participation in the first two surveys. If your customers see definite improvements as a direct result of the feedback, you will soon get 100 percent participation.

On the next page is a sample of a survey designed for gaining insightful feedback from your internal customers.

Miguel, the director of the purchasing function for a large specialty manufacturing company, received bad news in his recent performance appraisal from the CEO. He lost out on his bonus and a raise because the CEO had received numerous and ongoing complaints about Miguel's team's service from several managers and directors.

Since he loved a challenge, rather than accepting the situation, Miguel bought several books on customer service and studied them.

Internal Customer Satisfaction Survey

Internal Department being Surveyed ____*Accounting Department*____

Date of Survey ____*June 15, 200x*____

Survey Conducted by ____*Purchasing Department*____

Summary of our Relationship as Supplier and Customer

The accounting department uses purchasing department to satisfy our needs for copier and computer paper. The accounting department requires that purchasing provide the correct account codes and prices on all purchase orders they issue.

Instructions for 1-4

Please respond to each need by checking off the most appropriate response

	Critical	Important	
Unimportant			
1. Need for accuracy in our work?	☐	☐	☐
2. Need for timeliness in our interactions with you?	☐	☐	☐
3. Need for responsiveness in your requests from us?	☐	☐	☐
4. Need for open communication with each other?	☐	☐	☐

Instructions for 5-12

Using the scale below, indicate your degree of satisfaction with the overall services we provide you. Please enter how you feel in the space to the left of the question.

Scale: 1 = Very Satisfied   2 = Satisfied   3 = Dissatisfied   4 = Highly Dissatisfied

____5. How satisfied are you that the information you now receive from the purchasing group is what you need to run your department?

____6. How satisfied are you with the various ways we communicate with you?

____7. How satisfied are you with the various ways we support your goals and mission?

____8. How satisfied are you that you understand the information we provide you now?

____9. How satisfied are you that you can use our services to manage your department?

____10. How satisfied are you with the promptness of our response time when a problem arises?

____11. How satisfied are you with our courtesy and helpfulness to your employees?

____12. How satisfied are you with our ability to meet your business information needs?

Even though they were all written for the external customer, he saw the connection to his situation. Each book emphasized the importance of being in touch with the needs of the customer.

With his leadership team, Miguel crafted an extensive survey. The first draft was nine pages. Before issuing it, they tested it with the accounting department. Miguel's team saw that they needed to shorten and focus it more. Once they were satisfied with the revision, Miguel met with each department that used purchasing services, and he explained the survey and its purpose.

Despite much skepticism (his customers doubted that anything would change), Miguel's team received more responses than they expected. After sorting through the responses and tabulating what was on their customers' minds, Miguel boiled the issues down to four policies that accounting wanted purchasing to put in place.

1. Respond in a timely manner to phone calls and e-mails.
2. Reduce the number of forms needed to get anything purchased.
3. Keep people informed on the status of certain requisitions.
4. Integrate purchasing records with those of accounting.

Based on this survey and further discussions with their customers, Miguel's team made the following changes, which radically improved their relationships with each user department:

✓ Implemented a policy of less-than-four-hour response time to all calls and e-mails.

✓ Implemented the use of purchasing cards that were issued to all users for their smaller purchases.

✓ Reduced the number of forms per requisition and put the forms online.

✓ Placed the status of all major purchasing on the intranet (so the person needing the item could access the data) and updated this information once each day.

✓ Using the survey on page 179, design your own internal customer survey. (You have permission to copy this form and adapt it for your own internal use.) Think about your services from the customer's point of view. Decide what information you need to measure how well you are satisfying customer needs. Remember to use the KISS principle for your survey — keep it simple, sweetie!

✓ Hold a super service summit meeting with leaders from all the internal support functions. Ask each team to give a presentation on ways that they are trying to improve the quality of their services and ways that they currently measure satisfaction.

As a united group, select two to three company-wide metrics that widely measure all internal support. Decide on practical ways to capture and evaluate these metrics. Provide a report to each department monthly, and use the results as an agenda item for your next super service summit.

Internal Support Metrics

Cross-functional meetings that start on time
Employee satisfaction or morale
Turn-around time (responsiveness) to calls and e-mails
Cycle time on key internal processes
New process or procedures implemented that reduce internal
paperwork

Step 5-1/2 — Get Started Today

Behaviors that get measured get managed.
Behaviors that get rewarded get repeated.

This last step in the overall strategy is up to you. You now have several specific actions you can take that will result in immediate improvement in the level of internal customer support you provide.

But change takes time. It is easier to continue to do the same bad habit than it is to learn a new behavior. So you must start the improvements today and constantly reinforce and measure them.

Transforming a culture takes time. The more entrenched the cultural norms, the harder they are to replace. It takes from eighteen months to six years to completely transform a firm's culture so that the new behaviors are integrated in employees' everyday actions and decisions.

Take heart. The sooner you start, the sooner your internal customers will see the fruits of your efforts.

Here is a list of pitfalls to avoid and recommendations to speed your journey:

✓ Don't expect lasting changes to happen quickly. Give yourself and your people time to learn.

✓ Don't expect your goal for getting to super service to work exactly as planned. Every organization is a dynamic and organic entity. For every change for the better made, something else changes for the worse.

✓ Don't focus your change efforts on only one department or function. Every employee needs to invest in the plan for super service. Your job is to sell the vision of what is possible when everyone makes an individual and united effort.

✓ Don't fail to recognize and reward each improvement, no matter how small. Big changes come only from small day-by-day and hour-by-hour improvements.

✓ Don't be afraid to hold people accountable for improving their service to each other. In nearly every business organization, one bad apple can spoil the whole bunch. People are smart, and they know who the disrupters are and who is demonstrating commitment to super service. Make it safe for employees to bring to light those people and areas that are creating obstacles to super service.

Once You Believe, It Will Be.

You must believe that you can create super internal customer service. It is not impossible, nor is it easy. It is, however, very profitable and rewarding for you. The stronger the inside support is, the better your service to your external customer is. Happy customers willingly give you their money for your products and services.

We all want each of our customers and clients to say, *"I love doing business with you because you make it so easy for me to get what I want. Thanks!"*

That is what I, as your coach, want for you too!

ABOUT RON RAEL

Ron Rael is an authority on transforming corporate cultures. As an executive for several innovative northwest companies, Ron established his expertise in building corporate cultures that emphasized extraordinary customer service supported by superior teamwork and employee loyalty. Ron Rael is an award-winning speaker, trainer, and facilitator. He applies proven advanced learning techniques that deliver bottom line results. Ron's custom-fit training and coaching enhances the effectiveness of people from top to bottom of an organization. He facilitates "Fast Forward" corporate culture, change, and mentors visionary leaders. A variety of clients including corporations such as Starbucks, Marsh McLennan, Costco, Albertsons and Premera Blue Cross; governmental agencies such as the US Navy and the Social Security Administration, and numerous associations partner with Ron to transform their workplace cultures.

Contact Information:
Ron Rael
549-227th Lane, NE
Sammamish, WA 98074-7141
Phone: (425) 898-8072
Fax: (425) 898-8902
E-mail: Ron@ronrael.com
Website: www.RonRael.com

CHASING CUSTOMERS
IS LIKE HERDING CATS...
Why Attraction is the
Heart of Customer Service

by Edie Raether, CSP

S o much of customer service emphasizes the needs, values, and perception of the customer. Obviously, getting feedback from our clients and customers is essential, but I'd like to introduce another perspective, not to replace but to embellish upon the more traditional notions of how to provide outstanding customer service. In my book, *Why Cats Don't Bark*, I discuss the heart of peak performance through change from the "insight" out. The answers do lie within, yet learning to access that inner knowing, wise-mind, or intuitive intelligence seems to remain a mystery for most people. The same principles of emotional and intuitive intelligence that increase peak performance are also effective in improving customer service. In addition to understanding the customer's needs, wants, and perceptions, you must also become clearer on your "internal stuff." Once you are crystal clear on your personal and professional or business mission, you will attract customers who share the same core values, creating a personal alignment, synergy and other positive elements of a relationship. You will develop a synchronicity that motivates and invites rather than chases and captures.

Whether we are discussing stress or time management, sales, marketing, or customer service, we are all given only so much time, energy and money, which is often a reflection of how our time and energy have been spent. Rather than frantically chasing after every waving flag disguised as opportunity, I am suggesting a more centered and focused approach that creates natural synergy and alignment. The latter obviously produces greater results and success with less effort and time. It's the old 80/20 rule in action. If 80 percent of your business comes from 20 percent of your customers, how are you productively investing that other 80 percent of your time? We all know that if you hire the right people for the right job, their performance will be outstanding and they will be your most loyal employees. The same is true with customer service. If your service or style of service is not what the consumer wants, you will never be good enough. You can't drive a square peg into a round hole! As you become clearer on who you are, what your mission is, and whom you best serve, customer service becomes a natural by-product. This strategic alignment is the foundation of all business success. It's based on the laws of attraction: people love to buy but hate to be sold. In the field of marketing, the books on positioning by Jack Trout and Al Ries and research on branding illustrate the power of clarity of image as opposed to marketing mania.

By dissolving differences and focusing on a common ground, a deeper connection evolves through a sense of cooperation and collaboration. When you stay "in tune" to your customer's expectations, you stay in alignment. People's needs may remain quite consistent, their expectations vary with perception. For example, a customer's expectations of service and amenities are not the same of a Motel 6 as they may be for a Marriott. Nor do customers expect a discount store to provide the same level of service as Nordstrom's. From Southwest Airlines we expect lower prices and understand that, in exchange, we forfeit a few amenities, such as reserved seating and meals. It's all about alignment. You may have a great product and superb service, but if it is not consistent with who you are or what you promise, and thus what your customers expect, they will move on. Reality isn't real, expectations are. Make no casual commitments.

There must also be congruency between what is efficient and what is effective. Traveling efficiently at 70 miles per hour but in the wrong direction is not effective. Another example of good intention and process but unfulfilling results is climbing the ladder of success only to realize that the ladder has been leaning against the wrong wall. What is your direction, mission and vision, and who are your ideal customers? What are you doing to focus and attract that perfect customer who shares your core values and competencies? You can't hurry love nor can you force "chemistry" or romance. Some things just click and some things seem to naturally repel. Your job is to use good judgment and wisdom in determining with whom you connect best and synergize. What is your market and whom might you best serve?

Customer expectations are both vertical and horizontal. A lateral expectation is not about the level or degree of service, but the type. It is about "what" service is rendered. For example, if a customer is more concerned about saving time, not money, and you are taking more time in order to save that person money, you may be projecting your values into the situation and not hearing what is requested. Vertical expectations are focused on "how" the service is performed and the process or degree of excellence. Once you are clear on the customer's intention, then your attention to detail makes the process complete and successful.

It's all about detail. When comparing the quality of one suit to another, the details are like a subtle magnet drawing us into a purchase. Although God is in the details, so is the devil. Your level of perceived excellence and service will be determined by your attention to detail, which is always a reflection of your intentions. In gift giving, we often excuse inexpensive gifts with the assurance, it's the thought that counts. Our thoughts are our intentions and desires, which ultimately transform potential into performance. Even in the severity of murder, we assess charges of first, second, or third degree murder by what the jury determines as the intention, such as whether or not the act was premeditated.

Not only in customer service, but also in every element of what we offer, our state of mind, thoughts, intentions, and heart speak all determine the quality of results and outcomes. For example, when the forever best seller, *Chicken Soup for the Soul*, was being written, no one with a negative mindset was allowed to contribute or work on what manifested as perhaps the best-selling series of books of all times. What might this same approach and philosophy do for you?

To know if you are really "in sync" with your customers, as in dating and your personal relationships, you need to have a courting time. You don't buy a car without a test drive nor do you buy a suit or dress without trying it on. In a similar way we need to court, test-drive, and try on our customers for a proper fit. Likewise, they need to try us out before making a commitment. Our perspective of our potential customers and their view of us is different looking at us from the outside. We get a different sense of how things feel when we try it on and get a perspective from the inside out, which is why we call it "insight." The inner vision provides a greater understanding and feel for fit. That doesn't mean there will be no need for future alterations to change with the times, but it does provide a solid start. Just as your employees do a better job when they love their work because it is a good fit, so also the right fit with your customers will provide a basis for success.

True customer service is about making one decision at a time, both in whom we attract as customers, whom we keep as customers, and how we realign ourselves when we get out of sync with them. If you religiously follow the policy and procedures manual and worship rigidity, your robotic style of customer service will lack human touch and intelligence. A situation which illustrates the cost of such inflexibility occurred when a large group of us had a close connection at the airport in St. Louis. Although time was of the essence, we all politely sat on a shuttle, waiting several minutes for it to depart to the other wing of the airport where our flight would be leaving in just minutes. Like well-conditioned mice, we all respectfully and passively waited for the shuttle operator to turn the key. Finally, I got up and confronted the driver with the seriousness of the situation, pointing out that, if she did not leave immediately, the airlines would lose thousands of dollars housing all of us for the night due to the fact that we were about to miss our connecting flight. The response I received indicated the shuttle left every fifteen minutes as if it were on an automatic timer, and there was no choice or hope for human intervention and intelligence. There seemed to be little concern that we would all miss our flights even though it was 11:00 p.m., and there would be no more connecting flights requiring the shuttle service. Having little patience for such a display of cerebral breakdown, I became quite proactive in the pursuit of the lost art of common sense, convincing her that logic should supercede the rules. She finally decided to deliver us to our destination. Only the physically fit were able to make their connecting flights. Unfortunately, the driver was caught up in the fear of losing her job should she bend the rules. There can be no logic to your service unless you empower your employees to, above all, use their heads! Actually, it was not just the shuttle driver who was programmed to passivity, but all of the passengers who felt so totally helpless — they simply resigned themselves to a phantom impossibility. The point is that most outrageously positive customer service is simply making good judgments and decisions which may require more than mechanical analysis.

Objectivity makes good sense in math but is deficient in the service industry. It is essential that our decisions and responses to each and every situation be a balance of input from both the head and heart. We need to pay attention to the sensory feedback our body gives us, which is often a gut feeling, also known as intuition, direct knowing, or unconventional wisdom. All hybrid decision-making requires a development of our intuitive sense of what is right and wrong. Much more sophisticated than a computer, the mind weighs the emotional pros and cons from our emotional memory of past experiences and provides feedback via a hunch or gut feeling.

John Seely Brown, director of Xerox Corporation's Silicon Valley R&D facility, made it clear that rather than a high IQ or GPA, he looks for people who have grounded intuitions and a passion for making an impact. Thus it's essential not just to attract our perfect customer with whom we can create a natural synergy and alignment, but also to choose the appropriate people as employees. Hire for attitude and teach the skills. To provide service that is in sync and in alignment with your customers, you must first hire employees who have personal alignment and self-awareness. You and your employees must be aware and conscious of your own thoughts, feelings, and actions and how they affect others. Our actions determine the response we get, and, in attempting to realign ourselves with an angered, dissatisfied customer, it is important to remember that what we give out is what we get back. Emotional management is crucial to maintaining a symbiotic relationship that is mutually satisfying and beneficial.

Where attention goes, energy flows. Your thoughts are the seeds of the realities you create. We previously discussed the importance of knowing the customer's expectations as their reality. It is essential to know and understand your own expectations, which must be purely positive for positive outcomes. An obstacle is something you see only when you take your eyes off the goal. "As you sow, so shall you reap." Studies with sales people have demonstrated as much as a 37 percent increase in sales when they were conditioned to expect "yes." Expect that every crisis is an opportunity in disguise. Always seek what you can learn from every experience. There is a Zen saying that "All experience is education for the soul." No one is your enemy, everyone is your teacher. Expect all breakdowns to be breakthroughs. Expect a miracle!

Self-awareness is a prerequisite for empathy and compassion, which Daniel Goldman refers to as our social radar. He states the key to knowing others' emotional terrain is an intimate familiarity with our own. Empathy is not only reading another's emotions, but also being able to sense and respond to unspoken concerns and feelings. Lacking such sensitivity makes us emotionally tone deaf. Anybody who thinks customers aren't important should try doing without them for ninety days! While computers may offer economic efficiency, they have no soul. They do not feel and have no emotion and thus cannot motivate or be motivated. With the primary needs of many customers being interaction, participation, inclusion, and affiliation, customer care will always require just that . . . care. Computers compute, but only people have the capacity to care.

Since even good marriages will have a "falling out" from time to time, so, too, we may fall out of alignment with our usually in-sync customers. Here are a few tips for getting back in sync, creating an even stronger bond, connection, and loyalty.

- Listen. Listen. Listen. Your silence speaks.

- Be attentive. Affirm and validate them. Offer empathy and understanding. See their concerns through their eyes, hear with their ears, and feel with their heart. It's difficult to sustain anger when you are both in agreement.

- Resist the temptation to defend your point of view. They will not hear a word you say until you have first given them your ear and your understanding. In fact, an early defense will only escalate emotions and increase the intensity of their anger. You want to open doors, not build walls.

- Become "one" with them. Use "we" language to regain a sense of alignment and reduce polarity and opposition. Stand side-by-side to suggest a buddy relationship rather than a position of direct opposition. Your body speaks!

- Ask questions that direct attention to solutions and problem-solving rather than allow customers to wallow in unproductive anger, conflict, and negativity. Again, ask what "we" can do to solve the problem and create a united front. It invites them to participate and thus feel more empowered, transforming blame into a mutual sense of responsibility.

- Reframe their perceptions. There are two sides or pros and cons to every situation. For example, if someone is angered because the wait has been long, acknowledge those feelings to get in sync and alignment, and only then suggest the positive

perspective of the same situation, which may be that it takes
time to give customers the attention they need. You may even
wish to get their permission before offering your suggestions.
It is more difficult to refute that to which we have concurred.

- When in a hole, rule number one is . . . don't dig! Never lie.
  People are forgiving. Ask for forgiveness rather than offer
  phoney excuses that may force customers to seek justice by
  creating bigger traps. The nation forgave Betty Ford for her
  alcohol dependence and your disgruntled customers will
  forgive you, if you ask. Lies not only cause people to feel
  betrayed and deceived but erode all trust, which is the glue
  in every type relationship.

- Ask them what they would do if they were you. Role reversal
  allows them to see with your eyes, hear with your ears, and
  feel with your heart. It invites them to understand you,
  empathize with you, and become one with you. What goes
  around comes around. If you recall, one of the first points I
  made suggested that you see the world, and specifically their
  problem, through their eyes.

- If the answers lie within . . . so do the solutions. However, you
  must ask the right questions. I would recommend asking your
  disgruntled customers, "What would you like me to do?"
  Simple questions often yield profound solutions and resolution.

- Love your customers and they will love you. We all mirror
  each other. If you want it, first you must give it. Having lived
  in Green Bay, Wisconsin, home of the infamous Green Bay
  Packers and cheese heads, I have witnessed customer loyalty
  and enthusiasm at its best. Their zealousness is second only
  to the excitement of the Badger fans at the University of
  Wisconsin where, win or lose, the fifth quarter is always a
  celebration. Milwaukee, Wisconsin, is home of another group
  of fanatically devout fans. If you don't own the "hog," you

don't own a motorcycle, according to customers and family
of the Harley Davidson clan. Talk about kinship. Every size,
sex, and sector of humanity is represented in this loyal group
of fanatical fans. They all own, drive, and love their Harleys
and religiously celebrate a very special common bond. Now
that's turning your customers into raving fans! By the way,
there is a shortage of these machines so if you want to join
the club, you will have to take a number and wait your turn!

Customer service is thus much more than giving service, it is about
being a servant. Service is a transient act, while being a servant is a state
of mind and a way of being. It reflects more than core competencies and
skills; it integrates core values and the soul of your service. What is your
core ideology? What do you stand for? Phrases like "mark my word"
and "you have my word" along with a handshake were once honored as
if written in stone or sworn on a stack of Bibles. Perhaps we need to get
back to the basics such as *please, thank you, be polite* and other good
manners. A personal benefit of please and thank you is that please helps
us clarify and focus on what we desire, and thank you maintains an
attitude of gratitude, which supports a feeling of abundance and attracts
prosperity. We also need to bury blame and resurrect responsibility.
Remember, even though a situation may not be your fault, it still may be
your responsibility to fix it. Honor also needs to be revived. Try greeting
each and everyone you meet with a sense of reverence, regard, and
respect and begin to make miracles. All change begins from the inside
out. It all begins with you. It's your call. Life is a feast and most poor
fools are starving.

Opportunities are everywhere. Chasing customers is like herding
cats. Peter Drucker states the purpose of business is not to make a sale,
but to make and keep a customer. In other words, when the sale ends,
the selling begins. Customer service is selling with integrity and making
a commitment to the relationship. When Vince Lombardi said,
"Winning isn't everything, it's the only thing," he was referring to

football, not customer service. Customer care is not about competition, but cooperation and collaboration. The rules in sports are not universal laws. Know your game, the league you're in, what balls you're hitting and where you want them to fall. Be a risk-taker, not a risk-wisher who merely goes with the flow. A risk-taker creates the flow. Unlike a couple of decades ago, bigger is not necessarily better or more beautiful. Stay in your niche to avoid the ditch! Know who you are, what you want, and whom you want to attract as customers to best fit your niche. Believe in yourself and your customers will trust and believe in you. Lombardi also said, "Confidence is contagious. So is lack of confidence." How we view others is a reflection of our own thoughts, feelings and behaviors. All change begins from the "insight" out. Ignite your intuitive intelligence and tune into your wise mind to hear your inner voice of wisdom and direct knowing. The choices are yours. As Kenny Rogers sings in *The Gambler*, "You've got to know when to hold them, you've got to know when to fold them, you've got to know when to walk away and know when to run. Knowing what to throw away and what to keep. Every hand is a winner."

Honor the winner in you, the winner in your employees or internal customers, and honor those customers who give you life — and your job! A greeting from India, namaste, sums it all up. It means the light, the love, the God in me greets the light, the love, the God in you. *Namaste!*

ABOUT EDIE RAETHER, CSP

A change strategist and human asset manager for over 30 years, Edie is a nationally-recognized authority on people and performance. Her mind-empowering strategies provide the power tools for mastering change from the "insight" out, transforming untapped potential into peak performance. With primary expertise in practical intuition, instinctual and emotional intelligence and thinking/behavioral styles, Edie's refreshing approach inspires action. Whether it is a seminar on leadership, team building, change, customer service, negotiations, sales, marketing or safety and stress management, Edie's motivational systems will fire 'em up! A restructuring-recovery specialist, her "thrivership" programs empower the working wounded to restore morale after crisis or layoff. More than 2500 professional associations and Fortune 50 companies have been empowered by Edie's keynotes, seminars, and follow-up coaching for sustained peak performance. Her clients include IBM, S.C. Johnson, J.C. Penney, Oscar Mayer, Marriott, General Motors, and Meeting Planners International. Edie has shared the platform with other celebrities such as Tom Brokaw, Patch Adams, Art Linkletter and Bob Hope.

Contact Information:
Edie Raether
Performance PLUS
4717 Ridge Water Court
Holly Springs, NC 27540
Phone: (919) 557-7900
Fax: (919) 557-7999
E-mail: edie@raether.com
Website: www.raether.com

LEADERS AS SERVANTS

by Frank Polkowski

You know me, I'm a nice person. When I get bad service, I don't complain, fret, or criticize. I wouldn't dream of making a scene. I just happen to be one of those nice customers. But I'll tell you what else I am. I'm the customer who doesn't come back. Oh, I'll take whatever you give me, because I know I'm not coming back. I might even argue with you and feel somewhat better by causing you grief, but in the long run, it's just better to leave and leave quietly. You see, a nice customer like me, multiplied by others like me, can bring a business, yes, even your business, to its knees. There are many of us. When we have received enough bad service, we go to one of your competitors.

As you may have heard, we are now in a period when companies that perform service rather than produce goods are increasing in profitability, size, and number. With this shift, customers, more than ever, focus on service quality almost as much as they do price. For the first time, in 2002, a service company, Wal-Mart, has been ranked as No. 1 in the Fortune 500. Improving service is the reason you chose this book. This chapter explores how you can make service a leadership behavior in all your people and help your leaders serve others.

Leader-Servant Posture

Before we talk about the Leader-Servant posture, think of your own organization. More specifically, step back and think of this and other organizations you are involved with, maybe as a volunteer or board member. Non-profits have many of the same issues we have, but we don't always think of non-profits as businesses. What attracts their new customers? Are there any similarities between your current organization and theirs? How do you make the customer "yours"? What brings your customer back? What brings any customer back?

Close your eyes and relax for a moment. Picture your people, those who are involved with direct customer service. Do they deliver the customer service you want? Do they know demonstratively what that level of customer service is? How do they know what a Fantastic Customer Service attitude might be? Are your customers standing up and cheering for you and your service attitude? What about those who are not directly, but organizationally, involved; do they know what that attitude is? Is that attitude demonstrated to the world?

Those of us in management and leadership positions need to be Servant-Leaders. We need to be "Cultural Advisers." As cultural advisers we promote the culture of our organization, which, among other things, includes our customer service attitude. Therefore, we must be examples to our peers, upper management, and customers alike. Not only must we be examples, we must be approachable. Leaders who serve, by design, are approachable individuals. How else can we develop leadership skills in our people if our leaders don't share them? It is a well-known fact that the more attention you pay to a behavior, the more it will be repeated. A Leader acting as a Servant must be our ambition.

Some Leader-Servant Examples

I recently experienced an example of a solid leader-servant attitude at the opening of a new Perkins restaurant in our area. One full week before the restaurant was to open, the entire, newly hired staff reported to work. It didn't matter what the level of previous experience was. Everyone was in attendance. In that week, they learned about the Perkins culture, the serving style, the cleanup process, and even tasted the food that they were to serve to customers when the restaurant opened. Oh yes, they learned the operational rules they were to work under, but service was key. The startup crew included what the Perkins people call "NSO" or New Store Openers. These were experienced people from other stores who had a penchant for customer service, knew the processes, knew the Perkins culture and could act as leaders serving others. To say the process was successful is an understatement. On opening day, the restaurant was full of previous Perkins customers and the usual curious crowd. I was one of those customers from a previous Perkins city. By the end of their first week of operation, I had returned two more times for meals. Why? Because from my first experience, the restaurant delivered service as if I had been a customer at that restaurant for years. I was not alone. I saw many repeat customers from earlier visits that week. Isn't that the wish of any new business endeavor? A solid, running, revenue start! All because of positive customer service and, of course, a good product.

So where does Leader-Servant come in? The NSO, or New Store Opening personnel displayed a high level of exuberance and a positive, infectious attitude. Besides teaching the "rules of the road," their service activity was hands-on. They helped serve meals and clean up side-by-side with the new staff. More importantly, they mentored the new employees. I observed many times that the NSO people were smiling, courteous, and helpful to the "rookies." Do as I say, not as I do, isn't evident here. This is a true leader-servant posture.

In a similar observation with RSA, Remarketing Services of America, in Williamsville, NY, a suburb of Buffalo, I found the culture to be similar to Perkins; but the product, customer base, and customer-contact mechanism were totally different. RSA works with banks and other financial institutions to renegotiate automobile leases, generally at the end of the consumer's contract period. Their client base includes a number of major banks in the United States and many, many leases. RSA supervisors and managers act as Leader-Servants. They are, more specifically, cultural advisers promoting the RSA culture. To quote one staffer, "I am a cultural adviser." The "I" here is everyone in the chain. Employees are called associates. The organization uses a service-profit chain. They believe supervisors must be motivated to be able to deliver service to and for employees or, in this case, associates. When you deal with improving customer loyalty, not only can you maintain, but you can increase the revenue stream. You can do that only when your people believe in the organization. Management has to do more than just focus on daily operations. They must deal with people management, people development, and the meeting of employee needs. When you have all these support pieces, you can develop a cadre of people who will move mountains without question. RSA people are educated in dealing with internal customer service first. If they take care of their associates, their associates will take care of customers, and, of course, customers will pay the bills and take care of the organization. This attitude reduces staff turnover, allows predictive indexing, and allows a better coaching base. Consequently, the organization can develop and promote from within with more predictable results.

Creating the Leader-Servant Climate

Now that we have seen several examples of Leader-Servant climates, let's take a look at what you can do for your own organization. As you have no doubt experienced, as employee attitudes deteriorate, so do loyalty, performance, and commitment. This negative attitude is transferred to your customer and eventually leads to the loss of customers. Employee expectations are one of the key drivers of employee attitude. If expectations are established in a positive, assistance-friendly atmosphere, it is easier to reinforce the positive culture you are trying to establish or maintain.

Organizational leadership must be defined as including all levels of management, floor leaders, and senior staff. Floor leaders are those people who do not necessarily have the authority to make management decisions but are looked upon by others as the people who have the right answers and are generally more readily available. Floor leaders are just as important in developing a positive customer service attitude as any other leader in your organization. Unappreciated, they can make it more difficult to establish a positive customer support structure and can have a negative effect on employee morale. Support must come from the top, and it must be visible and demonstrative.

Support also must include senior staff who are not in management positions. For any organization to reinforce a positive, servant-friendly atmosphere, positive commitment from all levels must be evident and nurtured continually. Customer service and the Leader-Servant posture must come first. As an example, a factory in Canada was having problems with safety at all levels in one of their plants. We were asked to initiate a different approach. It was recommended that a "safety first" attitude was to be the rule. Therefore, safety must always be first in everything they did. This meant that on the front page of the employee newsletter there would always be an article about safety. All other printed material had an item about safety on the front cover. All doors and gates to their facilities had safety notices on them so they would be the first thing an employee would see upon entering the location. All meetings, conferences, and retreats included a safety skit or announcement. Safety truly was first. The number of safety incidents was reduced significantly within the first few months. Likewise, if Fantastic Customer Service is your goal, your leadership must be servants to the mission and all the people who support your organization.

Leader-Servant Shopping List

Just as you should never go to the supermarket without a shopping list, you should never establish a program or seek to create a climate without knowing what resources you have and what resources you need. To develop Leader-Servants, you need people who will share thoughts and processes; guide, but not dictate; ask "why" questions, and perform what Tom Peters, leading business author and founder of the Tom Peters Group, calls "naive listening." Naive listening allows the speaker to talk and make the point before you, the listener, answers. Many times we answer before the speaker is finished. Consequently, the same questions will be asked over and over again as we have stolen the opportunity to learn from the one asking the question. What, then, do you need to do to improve your customer service, utilizing leaders as servants? First, make a list of proficiencies you need. Gather active input from all levels of management, senior staff, floor leaders, and entry-level people. You now have involvement and ownership from all levels. Second, take inventory of the skills that you have, and identify the key players who can impart those skills to others.

Using the lists of "need" and "have," develop a training plan that:

1. Reviews the mission and goals of your organization

2. Promotes your service posture

3. Highlights the benefits of a solid service attitude to your attendees

4. Places attendees in energetic role-play situations

5. Allows for discussion of past service-related issues without reliving blame

6. Celebrates the positive impact of Fantastic Customer Service

Don't wait for everyone to be trained. Make your intentions known to all as you would any major announcement, but begin changing the atmosphere to a Leader-Servant climate with the first group.

Evaluating the Process

Now we must ask the question: are we experiencing leadership examples in areas we haven't seen before? If we are, we need to celebrate those positive changes and the people involved. Carrots have always worked better than sticks. If we see something that is good, we need to foster more of that activity — it's contagious. Is there a higher level of employee morale in the organization? If so, celebrate. If not, find out what's wrong. You have embarked on a mission to change attitudes and increase customer service levels. Are your leaders serving others? It is important at this stage of the game to analyze the changes in your organization and react. You need to demonstrate to your employees that you are involved, active, and caring. Otherwise, it may become a "flavor of the month" program and not become a constant behavior.

What if it doesn't work? How do you recover? As with any project, there will be successes and failures. The important issue at this time is to not give up. You still have the business to run and customers to serve; it is important that you make any adjustments so that they are transparent to the customer. If the customer becomes involved, apologize if necessary, but explain what you are doing. Very possibly, some customers could assist you in your project. You can learn from each other, and the interaction could be a very positive reinforcement to that customer's loyalty. Customers talk to other customers. Likewise, if your changes create some very distinct and positive customer relations, ask those customers for their opinion. They may be glad to help. Customer support and customer involvement with successes also breed customer loyalty. Again, customers talk to other customers.

Leadership isn't for everyone. Yes, it would be wonderful if all of your employees embraced your customer service strategy and your use of leaders as servants, but that doesn't always happen in today's world. Don't dismay. Rome wasn't built in a day. This change has become your policy. As with the restaurant noted earlier in this chapter, positive attitudes and exuberance breed positive attitudes and exuberance! What is important now is that management does not become transparent. Management transparency occurs when subordinates point toward top leadership as the reason why things change instead of endorsing the change and supporting it at their level. With continual nurturing, a positive attitude and a broadening of leadership at all levels will occur.

ABOUT FRANK POLKOWSKI

*F*rank Polkowski is president of NonProfit & Management Consultants, providing organizational consulting, strategic planning, and development programs for boards, management and staff in all aspects of non-profit organizations. He is a seasoned veteran with twenty-five years experience in strengthening both non-profit and for-profit organizations. A member of the National Speakers Association, Frank has delivered over 1,000 personalized keynote programs and speeches to audiences of all types and sizes, enlightening them in the finesse of improving themselves and their organizations. Frank is past president of the Buffalo Niagara Chapter of American Society of Training and Development. To stay current with trends and professional development, he holds memberships in the Society of Human Resource Management, the Association for Volunteer Administration, and BoardSource (formerly the National Center for Nonprofit Boards). He serves on several professional, cultural and civic boards of directors, further keeping his skills honed to current situations.

Contact Information:
Frank Polkowski
NonProfit & Management Consultants
6342 Pin Cherry Court
East Amherst, NY 14051
Phone: (716) 741-7403
Toll Free: (800) 610-6564
Fax: (716) 741-9735
E-mail: FCP@aol.com

TCIM SERVICES:
A Culture of Quality and the Right People Create Extraordinary Customer Service

by Linda C. Drake

My heart leapt to my throat. I stood — not as confidently as I would have liked — in the doorway of the office of our new company. I wondered how on Earth I would make this happen.

It was December 1987. Our first teleservices call center stood empty in front of me.

The Chestnut Hill Road office filled less than 4,800 square feet in a small commercial building in the shadow of the University of Delaware football stadium in Newark, Delaware. But the space those 40 vacant cubicles and chairs occupied seemed cavernous, just weeks before we were to start taking calls for our clients.

It was the first time I truly realized the scope of what I had undertaken. A curious mix of awe and self-doubt filled me that morning.

The feeling of angst had been growing in the months since my husband Tom, a DuPont Company telecommunications executive, and I first contemplated my departure from a wonderful and well-compensated marketing job at Blue Cross Blue Shield.

The anxiety spiked when I signed the lease for the space, wondering how I would ever make the monthly payment of nearly $2,000 to which I was committing. In my weakest moments, I wondered if I was putting at risk our home and our family, including my two young sons, one in elementary school, the other approaching it.

TCIM Services was founded in that spot that morning.

The TCIM Services Success Story

TCIM Services has grown to be the customer care industry's first ISO 9002 firm, and the industry's largest privately held woman-owned firm.

TCIM has won a number of awards in its 15 years in business, including the Torch Award for Ethics from the Better Business Bureau (BBB), the W.L. "Bill" Gore Award for Quality from the American Society for Quality (ASQ), and an entrepreneurial award from the National Association for Women Business Owners (NAWBO). Ernst & Young also named TCIM the Delaware Valley Services Company of the Year!

Today, TCIM Services, with its sister company LTD, is one of the industry's most successful privately-held enterprises. Our client partners are some of the world's largest companies, for whom we provide "extraordinary customer service" to their important customers. To our clients' customers, we are transparent, conducting our work 24-7.

But that December morning in 1987, I've long felt, was the beginning of our journey. And, it was not me who made TCIM Services such a successful company.

Rather, it was the "extraordinary customer service" principles that I'd learned in my life and work that became the core business principles of TCIM. Our mission, unchanged since that day, is to enable our clients to achieve exceptional business results by delivering the best in service and sales performance.

We filled the 40 chairs, and we took care of our clients. Every day we learned something new about business, about people, about technology, and about customer service.

Success is in the TCIM Culture

My own corporate background at Blue Cross Blue Shield and

IBM, and Tom's professional background at the DuPont Company, had focused us on meeting customer needs. Our emphasis was on the relationship we established with our clients and the products and services we provided them in the context of that relationship.

In the process of building TCIM Services, we went through an enormous paradigm shift of our own. To win in this business — to provide outstanding customer service — meant that our people had to learn to work effectively with our clients' customers on their terms, not on ours.

This policy meant we needed to give up more control than perhaps we were used to giving up. It also meant we needed to rely on the quality of the people we recruited and retained, and on the processes and systems that we put in place to support and reward them.

Fundamentally, the new paradigm challenged us to be masters of change. We learned several lessons in the process that worked for us:

- We anticipated change as a process, working to understand it, manage it, and lead it, as it affected each of our people individually and our organization as a collective;

- We worked to foster change, encourage change, empower and reward change;

- We communicated effectively, through regular meetings and various media, to make our ideal performance standards the actual standards for each of our TCIM associates;

- Perhaps most important, we learned to listen more effectively to our clients and to our own people, who were in regular communication with the clients of our clients, which helped us align our performance with our clients' needs, wants, and values!

Today, we're still learning. We've grown from that 40-seat operation to a company that operates call centers throughout the United States and in Canada. We take pride in the level of customer relationship management services we have come to provide to our clients.

The customer care industry exists in a constantly changing environment. To succeed, you not only have to understand customer service, but also technology, trends, and best practices that re-invent themselves nearly every day. You have to be a learning organization!

In our view, we're preparing TCIM Services and LTD, and our people, for a customer service environment that will feature three important trends:

- Multi-channel access, including e-mail, web chat, web call-back, web collaboration, voice-over IP and voice-over net, such as the Interaction Center which TCIM has used to integrate various features with telephony;

- Personalization of each customer transaction and interaction, based on thorough customer knowledge; and

- Data management that features integrated knowledge management and contact management, in a way that enables our front-line employees to deliver superior service without fail.

In this dynamic industry, we learned fast to stay at the cutting edge. After 15 years in business, that's a lot of learning. We've learned from our trials and from our successes. Most importantly, we have learned, too, from our mistakes, our misses, and our failures! The constant process of learning makes a difference to our customers, and to their customers.

Shortly after that enlightening December day, we made a commitment to our clients. We are the clients' front line; our employees are their employees, so their customers are our customers. We think about that every time we answer a call.

Growing Pains Helped TCIM Succeed

In terms of business management, riding the tide of unpredictable market trends and our dependence on individual clients made for a rather unsteady growth trend. But time has proven that the key to longevity is sticking to your principles, no matter the circumstances. Our commitment to customer service helps our clients through the rough times, so they stick by us through ours. This is true for the worst of our moments, and each of those is an incredibly valuable learning opportunity.

In 1992, the United States entered the Gulf War, and the American economy was at a low-point. Our country was in shock.

What does that have to do with customer care? No one was doing business. Around the country, offices usually bustling with activity were now quiet, as employees watched the war live on 24-hour television. Our clients no longer wanted to call Americans at their homes to talk about new products and services. Their customers didn't call in to ask questions or sign up for the latest offer. Our industry was in trouble, and as a growing new company, still dependent on every client after less than five years in business, our livelihood was also in jeopardy.

TCIM survived that period and came out stronger on the other side because "business as usual" inevitably returned, and our customers needed their businesses brought back in a hurry. Staying committed to customer service, and the principles our business was built on, made us a sound investment and a reliable partner for our customers to come back to when it counted the most.

The lessons we learned from that experience were incorporated into the way we work, and they helped us be better prepared for similar situations in the future.

Following the tragedy of September 11, 2001, America again went into shock, and an already faltering economy really took a downward turn. Based on our experience from 1992, we were able to sustain ourselves through the worst of the recession. We communicated to our clients that we would respect their needs in these extreme circumstances, and that we would be ready for whatever they needed as soon as they needed it. And as business returns to normal, our clients are sticking with us, because of our performance and our ability to build relationships that last.

Milestones for TCIM Services

As with any venture, the path of growth or success is rarely a straight line from A to B, but a series of peaks and valleys that, over time, shows steady progress toward the goal. Of course, our growth is no different. Throughout our 15 years in business, we have not only learned from our hard times, but have had breakthroughs that are just as telling about the kind of business we are, and the kind of business we will become, as we constantly strive to improve.

In order to grow a business, it must be managed for growth. And, rather than manage the business in its current state, you must manage for the business you will become. We learned this lesson the hard way. It begins and ends with people. It is critical to have the right people in place before you begin to implement your strategies for growth.

Because people make the difference between good or bad relationships, and good or bad customer service, we invest a lot in our people. We are selective, we provide great training, and we give them all the support they need to do the best job possible. This policy pays dividends in small ways every day, but, on occasion, makes a visible difference that reinforces to everyone why we maintain these standards.

In 1994, we attracted a large telecommunications client who selected us for a short-term but high-profile program. In our business there are no small pieces of work, so we gave them the full extent of our commitment and resources.

One average night, the CEO of the client company called one of our representatives with a customer service issue. The representative handled the call, not knowing who was on the line or the critical nature of that information exchange.

Soon after, the CEO sent a message complimenting the extraordinary level of service he had received. The representative had been helpful, informed, articulate, and had represented his firm exceptionally well. Within a few weeks afterwards, the business opportunity with his company increased substantially.

It's a moment like that when you stand back and reflect on what success really means to you and your business. While there is always room to grow and learn and improve, moments like that give the invisible "pats on the back" that make the struggles worthwhile. I can remember thinking, "We must be doing something right." Now we strive for those moments with each of our clients, and build on each success.

Pearls of Customer Service Wisdom

In every industry, the crucial lessons that make the difference between success and failure may differ. In customer care, though, the same lessons apply to everyone, because satisfied customers make the difference between success and failure. Taking care of clients and their customers for the last 15 years, we have collected our fair share of wisdom.

One critical element of extraordinary customer support is our ability to share our clients' vision and to translate that to a systematic, comprehensive solution to their customer interaction needs. We have to know our clients so deeply that we can anticipate programs, training, technology, and staffing needs on their behalf without missing a beat.

We pride ourselves on keeping pace in this dynamic industry. With effective customer service, clients shouldn't hear about new developments in software, technology, or programming from anyone before hearing about them from us. We're looking out for their best interests . . . always. This kind of relationship establishes a level of trust that provides the flexibility we need to do the best job we can every time.

We have worked in the past with clients who came to us wanting exactly what they didn't need. Because of the relationship we had with them, we were able to help them design better programs that got great results. Sometimes clients confuse needs, wants, and desires.

As seasoned professionals in our industry, we must be able to sort through objectives and technologies to produce achievable outcomes. This is not possible unless we have established a relationship of trust with our clients.

Keeping pace, incidentally, is not limited to technology. Keeping pace with our customers' expectations and satisfaction is something we take very seriously. Recently, we conducted a large-scale research project to help us understand what clients are looking for in the ideal customer care firm. We found that the biggest differentiating factor was indeed high-quality customer service. This was no surprise.

Something in this research study did surprise us. A number of companies expressed an interest in doing business with our firm because we cared enough about their business perception to commission a project of that scope. They thought it said something about our principles. They were right.

People Are Our Greatest Business Asset

Our trademark is our people. We take very special care in choosing the people who join our team, and we give them everything they need to succeed. They are our greatest investment. Over the years that we have been staffing our business and promoting managers, we have learned to never underestimate the potential of people, especially if you support them as you should.

Mike Jones began for us as a Customer Service Representative (CSR) in Stillwater, Oklahoma, in 1994, his freshman year at Oklahoma State University. He stayed with us, loved his training, and took pride in his work. Mike today is the Vice President of Sales Acquisition.

Holly Beatty started in 1998 in one of our call centers. She showed such an affinity for customer service that she has also worked her way up with perseverance and a great work ethic, and Holly is now a Vice President in Account Management.

Holly and Mike are examples of the kind of people we like to develop, and of the ethic of loyalty that is one reason they have succeeded at our company. Their longevity with us, and our clients' longevity with us, speak to our core belief that people are our most important assets.

The Right Direction

The customer care industry has come a long way since we opened our doors. A paradigm shift has occurred, and at its root, you guessed it, is a commitment to outstanding customer service. Clients used to look at their call centers as cost centers, a necessary evil in the way they did business. Due to changes in technology and in the perception of customer relationship management, yesterday's call centers are today's profit centers. The bottom line to any client business is a satisfied customer.

The cornerstone of our business today is in the shift to "inbound" customer interaction, which has led to a need for highly trained relationship specialists who answer when your customers call with a question or a problem.

That's where we come in. Outsourcing customer care, especially in this economy, can relieve the burden of some of the client's overhead costs without sacrificing the necessary human resources.

Most client companies are now finding that inbound call centers pay for themselves, but only if leaders and teams make a commitment to service. The right program, the right people, and enough flexibility to represent the company make for a profitable center.

Previously, customers would call in to dispute a charge on their bills, register a complaint, or ask for more information. The call would be handled in the manner requested, and ended, often without any benefit added to the client's company.

Now technology enables our specialists to have instant access to important information about the caller. How many times have they called? Have they made complaints? What are their purchase habits? When was the last time they raised an issue? Was it resolved? The answers are at our specialist's fingertips.

Suppose your customer calls with a problem about his bill. Our specialist knows what service he has, for how long, and what other services he has. Of course we'll gladly take care of the problem, but then we can enhance client customer value by evaluating usage patterns, stating when applicable, "Based on your usage, perhaps this plan would work better . . ."

Cross-selling and up-selling to customers you already have, who call in to your company, are the best ways to generate incremental increases in sales of products and services. But it only works if the commitment to customer service goes beyond just answering a call. You have to invest in people who know how to listen and have the flexibility to problem-solve. And technology is making the second part much easier.

This is an era when the metrics and evaluation of customer relationship management are changing. Customer service is no longer about the length of the call or the dollars of product sold. Increasingly, there is a measurement for value.

Clearly, there is value to spending more time with a customer, if the result is increased satisfaction or the sale of an additional product. Certainly there is value in the call center that takes calls and develops lasting relationships with customers, just as there was value for the outbound center years ago.

Our industry measures that value in ways we never dreamed of before, thanks to technology. But the value is delivered through customer service. We can instantly provide reports to clients about the day's activity and get his feedback on our performance. This exchange of information makes a difference, especially if we use it as a tool for improvement.

Relationship Business

My point about customer service is that it's all about the execution of the highest standards and practice. And, it is about the relationships you have with employees, clients, suppliers, stockholders, and a hundred other groups in which a relationship helps maintain a successful business. It's my job to make sure everyone at TCIM understands how important these standards and relationships are, and how they affect what we do.

Periodically we sit in with our relationship specialists as they receive calls. As an observer of countless interactions, I can share with you the elements of the classic customer interaction:

- Each call is answered in a professional, friendly voice specifically asking how we may be of service;

- We encourage each customer to articulate the reason for the inquiry; we summarize the customer's statement, applying active, empathic listening skills;

- We demonstrate the responsiveness, capability, and confidence that results from in-depth training; and

- We work diligently to educate the customer regarding the steps we will take to resolve the issue, when it will be resolved, and check for common understanding of the plan.

As the customer care industry continues to evolve, many outcomes are unpredictable. You can be sure, though, that whatever the future holds for businesses in all industries, one of the cornerstones will be customer service that builds relationships.

As I look back today, reflecting on that December 1987 day that started this journey, I'm thankful that, in over 15 years, I have known the kind of people who truly add value to the lives of others. They are outstanding people in our companies and the wonderful clients that I cherish, and many other supportive individuals in the communities in which we work, and for our community at large.

ABOUT LINDA C. DRAKE

*L*inda *Drake is the founder and CEO of TCIM Services, Inc. TCIM is an information services company providing integrated direct marketing, supporting Fortune 1000 corporations. TCIM's services include inbound and outbound teleservices, direct mail, market research, database management, and online data systems. In recognition of TCIM's implementation of customer satisfaction measurements and internal quality initiatives, TCIM Services was selected as the first Delaware Quality Award recipient in 1992. Since that time TCIM has achieved ISO 9000 registration, the first teleservices company worldwide to do so. In March 2002, the Better Business Bureau of Delaware presented the Torch Award for Marketplace Ethics to TCIM. Linda is the recipient of numerous other awards, including the State of Delaware's 1994 Entrepreneurial Woman of the Year and the* Philadelphia Business Journal's *Women of Distinction Entrepreneurial Award. TCIM Services is also proud of receiving a 1994 MVP Award from* Call Center Solutions *magazine. In June, 1996, Linda was honored as Ernst & Young's 1996 Entrepreneur of the Year.*

Contact Information:
Linda C. Drake
TCIM Services, Inc.
1011 Centre Road
Wilmington, DE 19805
Phone: (302) 633-3028
Fax: (302) 633-3270
Website: www.tcim.com

FIVE S.M.A.R.T. IDEAS
FOR PLACING YOUR CUSTOMERS
AT THE CENTER OF THE UNIVERSE

by Doug Smart, CSP

Your customers are just like you when you are a customer. They want the transaction to focus on their needs and feelings. Their concerns — not the business's — are the focal point. In transacting business, they want to be in the center of the universe. Consider this. The last time you bought from a flower shop, was the main reason you chose to do business with that particular establishment because of:

    a. convenience?

    b. fair prices?

    c. excellent work?

    d. your need to enrich the owners?

As a business consultant, the only time I've heard someone pick "d" was because the owners were her parents. Chances are you chose to do business with your florist for reasons that centered on your needs not on the owner's needs. In that small business decision, as the customer, you maneuvered yourself into the center of the universe. The focus of the business transaction was on your needs and wants. How appealing would it be to you if the florist: 1. advertised their location as inconvenient because the rent was cheap, 2. their prices too high because they didn't have the willpower to control costs, and 3. their work uninspired because sticking flowers in a jar of water is no big deal? Basically they would claim the center of the universe position for themselves by communicating, "Here is how we do business. If you want to be a customer of ours you have to accept it." You would not voluntarily patronize it, because your needs would not be met. In other words, if the business focused on their needs, not yours, and they plopped themselves in the center of the universe, you'd be turned-off as a customer. And turned-off customers can be counted on for three things:

- They buy less, if at all.

- They are not repeat customers if the competition provides better alternatives (and failure to win repeat customers is a death sentence for any business).

- They badmouth your business, driving away potential business.

Here's an important tenet for success: Between the business and the customer, there is only room for one in the center of the universe. When the business claims the center position, the business loses. When the customer is in the center, the business has a chance of winning.

Frequently, shoddy customer service that drives you and me away is nothing more than the service provider focusing on himself and not on you or me as the customer. For example, while you are frantically looking for your purse, the pizza delivery guy hollers through your open front door, "C'mon lady! I haven't got all night!" Intellectually, you know his words are true, but emotionally, you feel antagonism because he focused on his plight and not your frustration. If he had said in an understanding tone, "I know you're trying hard to find it fast. Thanks. That'll help me make more deliveries tonight," you'd probably double the size of the tip to compensate him for his concern and trouble. All the savvy delivery person did in the second example was to put you, instead of him, in the center of the universe. What a difference in positive feelings that provokes in the customer. And customers love to do business when and where they feel good.

Here's another example: A new business installs a portable, changeable letter sign that flashes, "You've tried the rest now try the best!" That's a cute rhyme, but who's at the center of the universe? The business, not the customer. Why? The business is pounding its chest, proclaiming it is wonderful. But who cares? We expect every business to have high business self-esteem. If we thought they didn't believe in themselves, we wouldn't want to patronize them anyhow.

Through the years I've had co-workers with the attitude, "Look, I just want the customer to buy something so I can make my sale and get my commission. I don't want a relationship and I don't care if they are at the center of the universe. I just want money." How effective is that? Let me ask you, when you are the customer with a customer-service zero like that, even through the smiles and making nice-nice, can't you spot a phony who's pretending to care about you in order to hurry you up to buy something? Your radar knows the salesperson is putting himself, not you, at the center of the universe. When you cannot occupy the center, you feel uncomfortable, unappreciated, and maybe disrespected. And you don't feel any particular connection to returning there or recommending that business to others. The business loses in the long run.

When you are the customer service provider, here is why it pays for you to place your customer in the center of the universe. You win!

- Loyal customers come back, so you make easier sales.
- Repeat customers spend more money so you're better rewarded financially.
- You get referral business and they are sold on you before meeting you.
- Your income is steadier and more predictable.
- Your value in business is evident, appreciated, and compensated.
- Success draws success, encouraging more business to appear.
- Your career gets red-hot.
- Opportunities develop to take your talents in fresh directions.
- You rise faster to the top of your profession.
- People seek your advice. You become a guru to your peers.

Zig Ziglar, author of *See You at the Top*, says that if you help enough other people get what they want the world will give you what you want. How can you help lots of people get what they want? As you have business dealings with them, place each of your customers in the center of the universe. It is a smart way to do business.

Five S. M. A. R. T. Ways to
Place Your Customers at the Center of the Universe

Start by asking, listening and taking notes.

Do not wait for feedback to drift to you. Go find out what is working, not working, and how customers feel about things. Painted on the walls of the auditorium in the headquarters of Wal-Mart, the world's largest retailer, are these words of Sam Walton, the founder, "The key to success is to get into the store and listen to what the associates have to say. It's terribly important for everyone to get involved. Our best ideas come from clerks and stock boys." Walton appreciated the importance of talking with his front-line "associates" (as Wal-mart employees are called) for real-world feedback. It makes sense for you and me to listen to our internal customers (employees) and external customers (buyers). We should "get into the store" and listen to what the decision makers — our customers — have to say. When it comes to internal customers, it is smart to routinely solicit their opinions about what happens in the business. Ask them about trends and recurring frustrations. Ask what they think might be "broken." When it comes to external customers, it is smart to personally ask what they like about shopping with you and your competitors. Ask them what they dislike about you and your competitors. Ask how they feel about doing business with you as an individual.

More question asking and listening not only position the customer at the center, they also make sales. When our children were young, we decided we should have a great stereo at home. I knew it would be expensive. I'll confess, at the time there were no audiophiles in our house. Being a visual person, my strategy for educating myself was to make a few early evening explorations to stores that sold stereo equipment and to discover what features were available at different price levels. Then, after processing the information, I'd go back and buy one. At the first store, the two salespeople standing idly near the door looked in the direction of a pimply-faced young man and indiscreetly signaled, "You're up." He approached awkwardly, so I brushed him aside with a friendly, "We're just looking today." He asked what we were looking for and directed us to the stereo department. We walked on. He stayed behind.

It was fun wandering through a sound system playground, reading tags, pressing little buttons, and comparing values. Ten minutes later he appeared and started a conversation. He asked about the system we had currently and what was good and bad about it. He wanted to know what type of music we enjoyed. He asked what room the new stereo would be in and how big it was. While he was asking these questions in a friendly, non-threatening, conversational way, he started jotting notes about our wants on a yellow pad. After a couple of questions about price, I made it clear cost would definitely be an important factor, and he continued asking questions about our needs. He made recommendations but mostly asked more questions and made notes of what we said. It was as if we had asked the knowledgeable teenager next door for advice before we flung ourselves into the scary world of stereos. All the while he was capturing our thoughts on his yellow pad. I must admit, having the attention focused on us versus having the attention centered on selling the stuff on the shelf felt refreshing and reassuring. He was knowledgeable about sound systems, and I felt understood. Feeding back to me my concerns and frequently my very words, he guided us through the stereo department like a safari guide. The upshot of this retail drama is we left an hour later with a new stereo system.

As a follow-up note to this story: I have made a lot of money because of that stereo-shopping trip. His style of putting the customer at the center of the universe by asking questions and taking notes felt right. I started doing the same as a real estate agent and I developed a loyal following of customers who not only bought from me but also referred their friends to me because, as many of them said, I was "the only one who listened." Yellow pads became an important piece of customer service equipment. Three years after the stereo purchase, the trade association I belonged to awarded me life membership in the Million Dollar Club for consistent outstanding sales volume, and I credit much of that success to asking questions and taking notes.

Here's a second follow-up note: The stereo salesman and I stayed in touch. Fortunately for him, he enjoyed a healthy commission scale that rewarded his skills. Within a year he bought investment real estate through me, introduced me to his fiancée, and treated himself to a car with the shiniest, blackest paint job I'd ever seen (even though I suspect it was a used one); it was a Porsche!

The payoff for placing the customer at the center of the universe is a strong one, and a simple way to do it is to ask questions and take notes.

In my company, our first contact with a potential client is usually by phone. In the preliminary conversation I or my associates ask a lot of questions to find out if I am a fit for what he or she wants to accomplish. We take notes on yellow pads. This helps customers feel positioned at the center of the universe. The notes later help me develop my consulting and training strategy customized to the customer. We try not to ask "yes or no" questions because we want to learn where their heads and hearts are on their issues. Here are the main questions that work for my clients and me. These are asked conversationally and not as a grilling. As the conversation progresses, some of these are saved for later, and many are answered before being asked.

> What would you like to accomplish by hiring me?
> What are three of the largest challenges your industry faces?
> How about your organization?
> What keeps people from being as effective as they can be?
> Where do you see your organization a year from now?
> Three years from now?
> What changes is your business experiencing?
> How well are people adapting?
> What is something your team has done this year that you're
>   particularly proud of?

Who is your competition?

In what areas are you better than your competition?

Where is the competition gaining on you?

What keeps you awake at night?

If you were giving a talk on _____, what are three points you would want the attendees to be sure to remember long after the talk?

Who will be involved in the decision to hire me?

The conversation usually lasts 10 to 20 minutes, and I gather several pages of notes. My clients teach me what their challenges are. This gives me insight on how I can help their situation. And the potential client, comfortable at the center of the universe, feels heard and appreciates that he or she is working with someone who is positioning himself to offer fantastic customer service.

I just gave you examples of questions that work when selling an intangible, like training. But what kind of questions can you ask if you are selling a tangible product such as men's suits? How about:

Do you need the suit for a special occasion? How soon?

Where else will you wear it?

What business are you in?

What brands have you found fit most comfortably?

What brands don't fit?

What is your favorite color?

Any colors you dislike?

How do you feel about the new synthetic fabrics?

Do you wear your jacket buttoned or open?

Do you prefer white, pastel, or dark shirts?

What type of statement do you like to make when you enter a room — quiet dignity, head-turning, or somewhere in-between?

What is your price range?

What do you think of this shirt, tie, and belt combination with this suit?

Customers expect professionals to ask questions. Doctors ask questions and as patients we give answers. In fact, we'd distrust the professionalism of a doctor who didn't ask questions. Smart customer service people are professionals who ask questions. When you are the customer, and the above questions are asked in a caring, conversational tone and in an unobtrusive manner, would you feel you were working with someone better than average? Would you rate that person as someone who is going places in business? You bet!

Your Turn
Placing Your Customers in the Center of the Universe

List five questions you can ask your customers within moments of meeting so you can find their wants and needs.

1. _____

2. _____

3. _____

4. _____

5. _____

Maintain the Proper Perspective: Give in When it Makes Sense

Today is blistering hot, and after two days of being on the fritz, our central air conditioning is running again. My wife, Gayle, our two children and I have suffered two fitful, sticky, sleepless nights — plus, we have weekend house guests arriving tonight! The air conditioning worked as good as new after we had the unit serviced two weeks ago. The trouble actually started four days ago when we hired "Mr. Sparky, America's Favorite Electrician" to replace a bathroom circuit breaker that had gone kaput. After he left, the bathroom outlets worked fine but the air conditioning and the lights in the foyer didn't. We called immediately and the electrician returned within an hour. He said, "I got the lights back on but I can't figure out why the air conditioning doesn't run. It must be a coincidence. I guess you should call your AC company back. Maybe they can figure it out." Two days later the air-conditioning technician's test indicated the equipment was fine, but no electricity was getting to the unit. After simply jiggling the circuit breaker box in the basement, it started working. He didn't know why and didn't understand what he did that made it work. Fine. Concerned about the fire hazard of wires so loose they can be jiggled, Gayle called the owner of "Mr. Sparky" and asked that he send a senior electrician to check us out and that his company pay the bill for the air-conditioning service call his technician recommended. He agreed to have it looked into. In the meantime the air conditioning quit on us again.

Two days later the owner himself arrived to check out the situation. He determined the challenge was an aging, faulty circuit breaker, which he replaced, and then he presented us with a bill. Gayle, believing in fairness and in the old wisdom, "You don't ask, you don't get," clearly and confidently stated we would pay for material but not for labor since this should have been spotted on the first visit, and that we should pay only the wholesale cost of the material to compensate for mental anguish, plus we would deduct the cost of the air conditioning contractor's bill. "Mr. Sparky" started to protest and then smiled. "OK, that'll be fine," he said and genuinely added, "I want you to be happy." Gayle felt the situation was resolved fairly and to her satisfaction. We figure he knew he could have left with $175 more. He may also have realized there are 1,000 homes in our neighborhood and neighbors love to express opinions about who is and isn't good to work on our homes. Will we call him again? Yes, without hesitation. Will we recommend him to neighbors and family? Yes, because we believe the work is good and his attitude is customer-focused.

Maintaining the proper perspective helps keep the customer at the center of the universe. That's smart service. "The customer's always right" might be a tired old saying, but the reality of today's marketplace is it costs much less in the long run to keep a current customer than to get a new one. A top-notch motivational speaker, Mike Marino, who owned a successful retail business for over 20 years, says, "You can be right, or you can be happy." It pays to give in when it makes sense.

Your Turn
Placing Your Customers in the Center of the Universe

List five past situations in which you could have "given in" without giving the store away and probably would have gained a loyal customer.

1. _____

2. _____

3. _____

4. _____

5. _____

Always Create an Environment That
Places the Customer in the Center of the Universe

Another effective way to offer fantastic customer service is to create an environment in which the customer feels comfortable doing business with you. I was in a New Orleans department store during the week between Christmas and New Year's, enjoying the holiday music wafting about and the tranquil rest of a descending escalator ride, when I over-heard an upset customer shouting at a sales clerk. In the fur department at the foot of the escalator, a nicely dressed but hostile woman with a bulky fur coat draped over one arm was giving an employee a piece of her mind. And some of the language was brutal. Sensing an opportunity to do some customer service field research, I decided to shop in the fur department.

"You stupid people never get anything right! You ruined my coat! I want you to take this back, and I want my money now!" she bellowed. The saleswoman, also well groomed, maintained her composure. The look of concern on her face, the slight tilt of her head and almost imper-ceptible nodding indicated everything was registering. She did not speak words, but her face asked "What happened? Why are you this upset?" The customer was practically ranting. The saleswoman took a half step backward. The customer took a half step forward. The saleswoman took another small step backward and the customer closed the distance. She did it again and the customer followed. A couple more steps behind her was a pretty French-style desk with a commanding leather chair behind it and two small, fancy, French-style chairs in front. She sat in one of the fancy chairs and the customer lowered herself into the other. All this time the saleswoman was virtually silent, but her customer service mastery was evident to me.

The nasty customer was led to the desk and chair area, the proper place for conducting business. When the customer sat down, she lowered her tone of voice, too. When the voice lowered, the choice of ugly words dropped with it. Taking a chair beside the customer signaled, "I'm on your side," which helped to further defuse the tenseness of the moment. Sensing it was now time to do business, she started asking questions. She let the talking customer take the center of the universe position, this time with civility.

I eavesdropped as much as I could! In response to questions the customer spoke more rationally. Here are the facts as I overheard them. She had long dreamed of owning a big mink coat and finally bought one for herself as a holiday gift. When it arrived her excitement turned into crushing disappointment. One of the three initials in the embroidered monogram was wrong. Her coat was "ruined," even though she clearly gave the correct initials to another (not present) salesperson.

I knew that when the other salesperson was brought up the saleswoman had an easy opportunity to extricate herself from this encounter, but she chose to stay on course. She could have pitched blame on the other salesperson ("Yes, we've had problems with her before") or on the customer herself ("Let's just get the order book out right now and see what initials you gave us!"). Instead, she chose the high road. She apologized that an unfortunate mistake had occurred. She offered to have the monogramming redone. But the customer steadfastly refused because "patching it" would make it feel like second-hand goods to her. Like a friend, the saleswoman continued asking questions along the lines of, "What made you fall in love with this fabulous coat? Do you agree it was a good value? What will it take to make you absolutely happy with this coat of a lifetime?" The customer dropped her defensive posture.

She really wanted the coat. And I'm sure the saleswoman was savvy enough to understand that the customer was more in need of an emotional outlet than of having her money refunded. The result of this talk: The customer agreed to keep the mink if the store replaced the entire silk lining and embroidered a new monogram. They shook hands. As I see it, the customer service skill of the saleswoman created a win/win/win/win: The calmed customer made a rational decision to keep her coat; the store kept the income from a high ticket sale; the other salesperson collected a healthy commission; and the smart saleswoman further enhanced her value to the organization by turning a potential disaster into a stunning victory.

You and your customers win when you create an environment customers want to be in. Think about when you are the customer: Do you prefer to do business in places that help you feel calm and receptive or in those that aggravate you so much you feel perpetually defensive? Do you prefer to spend your money in businesses that adjust to your feelings or in those that make you contort to their rules?

Your Turn
Placing Your Customers in the Center of the Universe

List five things you can do to create a more customer friendly atmosphere.

1. _____
2. _____
3. _____
4. _____
5. _____

Remember: Don't Assume Customers
Know What You're Talking About

Sometimes customers do strange things because they don't understand what is said to them. *The Wall Street Journal* relates the following examples: Offering computer know-how via the telephone, a technical support staffer asked a customer to send a copy of her defective diskettes, and a short time later an envelope arrived with photocopies of the diskettes. Compaq Computer has discussed dropping the command "Press Any Key" and replacing it with "Press Return Key" to stem the barrage of calls for help finding the "any" key.

In the real estate business, just like in your business, we flung around "shop talk" words and phrases such as equity, debt-to-earnings-ratios and private mortgage insurance, as though everyone knew what they meant. The customer is not in the center of the universe if he or she cannot understand your language. It's smart to make communication easy for both the customers and you. Be certain you can be understood.

Your Turn
Placing Your Customers in the Center of the Universe

List five technical terms you use that have customers asking "what did you say?" Next to them list 5 phrases you can use instead.

1. _____
2. _____
3. _____
4. _____
5. _____

Try to Give Service They'll Talk about for Years to Come

There is an American proverb: "Everybody loves a winner." Delta Air Lines is fortunate to have a winner in flight attendant, Michael McGhee. He has the skill to put the customer at the center of the universe. A couple of years ago, on a cross country flight, he and I chatted about customer service. After a little prodding from me, he related the following:

"I was working in first class when a pocket of turbulence jolted the aircraft and sloshed red wine onto a passenger's white dress shirt. Instantly, he wiped at it furiously, but the cotton grabbed hold and the stain spread wide. He asked for my help. I had him go into the lav and remove his shirt. In the galley, I poured club soda on the stain to dilute it. This helped some, but it didn't really remove the stain, so I quickly searched my flight bag for something stronger. There's a new product available for lifting stains and it comes in small wet sheets in foil packets that you tear open so you can have one handy when you need it. I always travel with a couple of these in my flight bag; I used one on his shirt and scrubbed until, eventually, the stain did come out. Unfortunately, his shirt was now clean but a damp wrinkled mess. I passed it to him. He was grateful to have the shirt spotless because, he told me, he had an important meeting to attend upon arrival and wouldn't have time to go to a store and buy a new shirt. I knew I could do better than this. So, without hesitation, I reopened my flight bag and over his protestations I insisted he take the clean, pressed shirt that I was going to wear on day two of my trip. I directed him back into the lav to try it on. Luckily it fit and he was back in business. The problem was solved. He thanked me a dozen times.

"When he mailed my shirt back to me, he also sent a glowing letter to Delta commending the customer service rendered above and beyond the call of duty. It was really thoughtful of him to write, but I felt happy to have solved the problem for him."

We talked further and in response to many questions from me, Mr. McGhee divulged he has over 50 letters in his personnel file from passengers who have written Delta to articulate their appreciation for the great job he is doing. He told me, "It's nice when they take the time to write and give me a pat on the back to say 'thank you for a job well done.' Each year, when I have a file review, my supervisor remarks at what an achievement that is and how other flight attendants don't come close to acquiring such a level of letters. My supervisor also stated that in this world where everyone is in a rush, people rarely take the time to write. For me, it's just nice to get an affirmation that I'm doing my job well."

Be a winner. Try to give smart service they'll talk about for years to come. Go out of your way to provide outrageously memorable customer service. Why? See if you agree with these three reasons. You will delight the customers enough to encourage their repeat business. You will build a career on a solid a foundation. (Quick test: If you were Mr. McGhee's supervisor and the order came down to reduce the number of flight attendants, do you think you would release one of your star performers to the competition?) You will fall in love with your job — again.

Your Turn
Placing Your Customers in the Center of the Universe

List five things you have done that rate as above and beyond-type customer service they'll talk about for years to come. If you can't think of five in the past, list five in the future that you'll try so you build a reputation for fantastic customer service.

1. _____

2. _____

3. _____

4. _____

5. _____

Build your customer base and your career quickly by placing your customers at the center of the universe. This smart approach will help you avoid the common, business-eroding trap of shoddy customer service that drives away business. A simple-to-remember and easy-to-apply approach is to get S. M. A. R. T.:

Start by asking, listening, and taking notes.

Maintain the proper perspective; give in when it makes sense.

Always create an environment that places the customer in the center of the universe.

Remember: don't assume customers know what you're talking about.

Try to give service they'll talk about for years to come.

ABOUT DOUG SMART, CSP

Doug Smart, CSP, works with leaders and teams who want to build optimistic organizations and customer loyalty. Clients learn how to bounce back from setbacks, earn customer devotion, and increase business. Plus, they have more fun! Doug is a successful business owner and a former top salesperson who is authoritative and authentic. His daily radio show, "Smarter by the Minute," is heard internationally. He is a consultant, keynoter and trainer who has spoken at over 1,000 conventions, conferences, seminars, sales rallies and management retreats. Doug is the author or co-author of Thriving in the Midst of Change, TimeSmart: How Real People Really Get Things Done at Work, Reach for the Stars, Sizzling Customer Service, *and* Brothers Together. *In 1998 the National Speakers Association awarded him the prestigious Certified Speaking Professional designation. Contact Doug's office for an information kit on bringing The Get Smart Series to your organization.*

Contact information:
Doug Smart Seminars
P.O. Box 768024
Roswell, GA 30076
Toll Free: (800) 299-3737
Phone: (770) 587-9784
Fax: (770) 587-1050
E-mail: Doug@DougSmart.Seminars
Website: www.DougSmart.com

SYNTONICS RELATIONSHIP MANAGEMENT® IS THE STRATEGIC CORNERSTONE TO FANTASTIC CUSTOMER SERVICE

By Sam Waltz

"What about CRM software?" the technology vice president questioned me in a challenging tone, as I finished my keynote remarks at a senior energy industry conference in New Orleans a few months ago. "Don't you think that Customer Relationship Management (CRM) software is the key to achieving success in creating outstanding customer satisfaction?"

Really, I'd tried to finesse the issue of CRM software in my remarks for two reasons.

First, the audience was full of the senior technical types, MIS, IS, IT, engineers and other data and technical executives, for whom CRM software was intuitively and obviously the answer to their problem, or so they thought. Second, although it might not sound like it, I really respect the value-adding contribution of the variety of CRM tools with which I'm familiar.

"Software is the tactic, it's not the strategy," I told my questioner. "Software represents some embodiment of what we decide to do, once we've decided how we want to solve our customer service issues!"

"My respect is for your intelligence and wisdom in problem-solving to lead change, and for our collaboration, not for the genius-in-the-box tool that we buy for $1,995 or $9,995," I added.

"What's important is how you and your company create the ethical paradigm that governs how you interact with your important stakeholders. The transactional interaction — the customer service behavior — flows from that, whether it's being transacted by CSRs or by vice presidents."

He smiled, nodded, and sat down.

We met later, enjoyed refreshing beverages, and traded some war stories about solving customer service issues and creating customer satisfaction that differentiates one organization from another. I listened and learned, and emerged with a new respect for the demands upon the quantitative side of the organization in designing and implementing solutions.

My new friend seemed to listen and learn, too, as I shared some views rooted in my 'social sciences' professional upbringing in research-and-writing journalism, remediated by a nearly 20-year second career as a senior executive at DuPont, that bastion of extraordinary and successful technical thinking.

Now, in my third career at age 55, directing two organizations of my own, and having served as the CEO of the world's largest organization of strategic business communicators, I help organizations like my new friend's corporation navigate change by straddling, converging, and synthesizing the quantitative side with the qualitative.

We help our clients understand that the human dimensions — the behavioral dimensions — are the tie-breakers in creating outstanding customer satisfaction. The astute leader can design a winning approach to customer service by creating winning stakeholder relationship management strategies, processes, and systems.

In fact, it was not surprising when my phone rang within a week after I returned to my Wilmington (DE) office about 20 minutes from Philadelphia International Airport. It was my new friend calling to bring us aboard for a win-win consulting assignment. We joined him at his company, and, in less than 90 days, we'd helped him develop a strategic behavioral paradigm in which he could move forward to install new customer satisfaction CRM programs and services.

His company saw an immediate increase in its customer satisfaction metrics and the sales that resulted! It made him a hero at work, his company made him its senior vice president, and it thrilled us!

Behavior as the Last "Black Box"

Human behavior, in my view, is the last black box that science has yet to understand.

The fundamental laws of physics were discerned a few centuries ago. The dynamics of the universe have been mapped, too, over that period. Homeopathic and allopathic medicine together have given way in just a century to a modern medicine that is increasing the length and quality of life by knowledge, intervention, and wellness strategies. Even some heretofore unknown secrets of mammalian life have been answered in the past decade by genome research. Applied within the organization, as I told the Economic Club of Detroit in a speech a couple years ago, data processing in the last two decades has given way to IS, MIS, and IT functions, which increasingly are becoming knowledge management, all of which is headed by a CIO, CTO, or Chief Knowledge Officer. Bookkeeping and Accounting in the organization has given way to Finance, which is headed by a CFO. Even the Personnel Department has given way to Human Resources, headed by a Chief Human Resources Officer.

But the lack of a larger world view by which to understand and describe human behavior leaves the organization trapped in niche functional disciplines like marketing, PR, advertising, employee relations, or community relations.

The ultimate capital for any organization is the quality of its reputation and its relationships. Just ask the leaders of Arthur Andersen! Reputation and relationships are a product of actions and choices. Behavior is the sum of choices and actions, and it's driven by values, beliefs, attitudes, predispositions, and information.

Behavior remains that great frontier. Why do people act as they do? How does one influence how they act, as I call it, "to create desired behaviors?"

Society lacks a *Weltanschuung*, as Max Weber called it, a world view that assimilates what we know about behavior. What's lacking is the meta-behavioral philosophy, the big picture that describes the laws of behaviors and the dynamics of human interaction.

The really great thinkers in human behavior, Freud and Jung, date back almost a century. Contemporary thinkers on behavior tend to be trapped in pop science, which lacks the kind of scientific rigor that accompanies the understanding of the physical sciences, and is too often based on anecdote.

Our current thinkers are taking out bites around the edge, though, with development of strategies based on cognitive theory of how people learn. Some writers are merging primary science into larger theories, as Malcolm Gladwell did in his outstanding volume, *The Tipping Point: How Little Things Can Make a Big Difference* (2000). Gender science has been one of the most productive specialties in the last decade, perhaps helping us be better spouses or life partners.

If we cannot remedy the absence of a meta-behavioral world view, we have to use what we have to create a behavioral problem-solution paradigm. We have to adapt, to accommodate, and that's what this chapter is about.

Strategy: Research, Design, Implement and Evaluate

I do a lot of presentations on strategy, on developing strategy, on becoming a strategic thinker, and on creating vehicles for strategic problem-solving. From time-to-time, a younger person in the audience will ask me, "Sam, I really enjoy my work on the tactics, on the program development. But I'm really interested in becoming more of a strategist. How do I become a strategic thinker?"

"It really is easy," is often my reply, "just get grey hair!"

I don't mean to make light of that young person's plight, simply because it is so widely shared, and because I could have asked the same question at 25, or even at 30, and older.

Strategy is problem-solving. Becoming a relationship strategist —

whether in marketing or in customer service, which in fact are joined at the hip — requires some kind of paradigm for understanding behaviors. Within that, then, is the challenge of gathering information, organizing and synthesizing and assimilating information, aggregating and analyzing and disaggregating it, framing critical variable issues, and engaging a problem-solving process that discovers the creative solutions that will propel the organization toward its desired outcomes.

Syntonics® as Win-Win Strategy

Syntonics Relationship Management® is the core business process we use at the Atlantic Leadership Institute and Sam Waltz & Associates Business & Communications Counsel to help organizations navigate change and create win-win relationships.

The word syntonics is rooted in ancient Greek, and it meant "creating a musical harmony." If you imagine two or three of you (not me!) singing in a way that actively creates harmony, then, in ancient Greece, syntonics described your effort. In its etymological evolution, syntonics came to mean creating a linguistic harmony, that is, communicating in a way that creates shared meaning.

We already had created our win-win approach to relationship management as a strategic planning process, when I ran across that mention of syntonics about 8-9 years ago. It occurred to me that it would be useful to adapt an evolved concept of syntonics to brand our process.

Syntonics Relationship Management® is the active strategic planning process of creating a win-win alignment via management of relationships.

That is, by identifying the individuals and groups of individuals who are important to you as stakeholders, and by learning and understanding their needs, wants, and values, you are able to understand the potential for the convergence of your interests with theirs, to create a win-win exchange of value. In that context, then, you are able to design and implement a strategic relationship management process that creates win-win outcomes and moves you and your stakeholders towards your goals.

Sounds simple, doesn't it?

Maybe you want me to tell you that it's more difficult than it sounds. In some ways, perhaps, but, for the most part, Syntonics Relationship Management® is a very intuitive, useful, and easy process to learn and to apply. Like any kind of strategic planning, certainly it requires a variety of professional competencies to accomplish, but it is not some kind of rocket science.

Some colleagues in the planning, problem-solving, and customer service industry like to suggest that strategic planning is a great mystical temple, where access is limited to only a sacred and learned priesthood elite.

Not so! Strategic planning — although it is a competency skill set of its own — is not all that complicated. Whether in our business or personal lives, such planning consists of asking and answering three simple questions:

- Where am I?
- Where do I want to be?
- How do I get there?

The reflection and self-assessment that accompany asking and answering these questions, and the planning that follows, can alter the course of our lives. On the bulletin board next to my desk, I have posted for years the words of three great thinkers about the value of questioning and reflection.

It was Aristotle who wrote, "It was through the feeling of wonder that people first began to question."

Socrates, the progenitor of the great Socratic method, wrote, "Since the soul has learned all things, there is nothing to prevent someone from discovering all the rest, if they are brave and do not grow tired of inquiring."

Plato, who occupied a similar niche with Socrates among the great thinkers, wrote, "We will be better and braver if we engage and inquire than if we indulge in the idle fancy that we already know."

Relationship Audit in Research

Too many organizations focus first on themselves, on their own needs, on who they are, and what they sell. It's essential to know that, because each organization does need to understand and clearly articulate its ultimate objective. It's misleading, though, to make that the center of the universe.

To be effective in customer service and to execute a strategy of building win-win relationships, an organization needs to audit its relationships. Audit, of course, is a financial term that CFOs and executives will immediately recognize. An audit examines, verifies, and corrects.

This is an essential step. How can you devise a strategy to improve unless you know where you want to go? How can you know where you want to go unless you know where you are? How can you devise a strategy unless you have good information about the start point and the future point?

Mapping who your stakeholders are is a much easier task than most would imagine. Brainstorm it yourself, and within 15 minutes you can build a list of 25 stakeholder sub-sets of your population who are important to your organization.

Then, in terms of understanding how to move forward in this process, ask and learn about your stakeholders' needs, wants, and values, with particular attention to their relationship with your organization. Next, determine via the same process where you are now.

Some organizations use quantitative measures, which serve them well in measuring progress. We tend to use qualitative research because we feel it better informs us with regard to engineering behavior, that is, creating the desired behaviors. Such qualitative measures include interviews, focus groups, and case studies.

One major corporate client, a refinery with an environmental performance site emergency, asked us to assist in strategy. Our research led us to interview some 35 opinion-leaders in the client's community, ranging from elected officials to the president of the state university to the heads of the organized building trades union locals and many, many others. With their insight, developing a win-win strategy was not a complex undertaking, although certainly the implementation of that strategy required diligence.

Another client, a quasi-public authority, needed to expand a landfill. Yet, who wants a landfill located next to his neighborhood, or expanded, if it is already there? Achieving that expansion is a political process, that is an aggregation of consent among opinion-leaders. For that client, we arranged some 25 meetings and interviews to pre-sell the need for landfill expansion, prior to the client's public announcement, so no surprises were created and sensitive issues could be uncovered as early as possible.

Win-Win Outcome in Design

Once you are able to map your stakeholders and their needs, wants, and values, then you are better able to adjust your own organization's interaction with them.

Build a marketing continuum and look at the demands along various parts of that continuum. Awareness — How do you build it? Interest — How do you drive prospect interest? Desire — How do you move the prospect to becoming a client or customer? AFTO — How do you create the transaction by asking for the order (AFTO)? Service — How do you deliver the product or service to the client or customer? Customer satisfaction — How do you build a quality relationship?

Three recent case histories come to mind.

In one, for a major regional construction management firm, we did neutral, third-party interviews with the firm's major clients and targeted prospects. Based on about 10 one-hour interviews, we were able to map about a dozen key client values in the abstract — values such as safety, teamwork, predictability, and open communication.

Then, from those interviews, we were able to describe what the client saw when the value was manifested or realized. Finally, from that understanding, we were able to identify and describe the behaviors that the construction management firm needed to put in place in order to meet its clients' needs.

From that research and planning, a table like this emerged:

Client Benefits	Values	Organizational Behavior
No lost time/ wasted money	Safety	Design & follow safety processes
No surprises	Open communication	Effective interpersonal communication
Other benefits	Other values	Other behaviors

That's a very simplistic description of a fairly complex work product that we produced, but it conveys the point. Note, too, that once the client integrated this knowledge into the firm's work process, it could be used to create and manage expectations and, ultimately, to grow the business.

In this case, with our client, we reduced the results of our work to a simple table, printed it on parchment, and, at the beginning of a job, our client started the new relationship with a signing ceremony between the firm and its client. Ultimately, our client was able to use the table in marketing, to differentiate the quality of its work from the competition, and the firm's revenues doubled in one year.

In another case, a reserve unit of the U.S. military came to us with a strategic human resources issue. Attrition — which normally ran at about 10% annually — had doubled to more than 20% in the last couple of years.

In a military organization where preparedness for combat and combat support is the goal, trained personnel is its major asset, and training and experience is its major investment. The value of that asset was depreciating too rapidly, at risk of 100% turnover in a 4-5 year period, corrupting the ability of that reserve force to achieve its mission.

Our research included a number of interviews, but, most importantly, three days of focus groups with heterogeneous and homogeneous groups (officer and enlisted, senior and rookie, mission and support, gender and race). We identified eight reasons that caused a reservist to leave duty, most of which could be remediated. If we wanted to understand why reservists left, then we needed to know why they joined in the first place and why they stayed, so we focused our research on that, too, identifying five such reasons.

For the military client, we then mapped "the tipping point," which is the time in the reservist's career when the reasons to leave outweighed the reasons to stay, and the events that triggered the decision to leave.

From that process, we were able to design a number of intervention strategies, the sum total of which worked to create what we called a culture of retention, which the Commanding General and his staff adopted.

In another case, a major national corporation asked us to research its prospective clients to learn what it needed to do to successfully compete for new business in an industry where a contract meant tens of millions of dollars in revenues.

From about ten interviews with decision-makers among prospects, we learned (and in some cases confirmed what we knew intuitively) that the prospects talked partnerships and quality, but in a new relationship situation, lowest price was critical to earn their business. Once the business was earned through lowest cost (often having to buy the business initially through slim/no margins), then our supplier client had the opportunity to increase profitability by finding ways to add value and raise prices. If quality ever slipped, then the partnering was undermined and the relationship was vulnerable.

In collaboration with our client, we were able to map these dynamics in such a way that the client adjusted its business development philosophies and process.

Each of these three anecdotal cases is simplified and disguised somewhat, but, clearly, great value accrued to each client from learning how to create a win-win relationship with important stakeholders.

Excellence in Every Behavior

Ultimately, in order to succeed, strategy does not work without excellence in execution, that is, the effective management of the organization's interaction. On one hand, this is one of the areas that CRM wares so effectively help track. They contribute to the management of interactions, as well as to the management of data.

For one client, a legal information publishing company that delivers to trial attorneys and corporate counsel a searchable on-line data base of oral argument to the Court, we recently evaluated CRM products for the applications service provider (ASP) to design into the technology from the ground up.

Since we are not principally a technology consulting firm, we don't work with such softwares every day. We were struck by the variety, quality, and vastness of the offerings today. Although some firms clearly have emerged as leaders, certainly an almost infinite number of choices and configurations exist.

On the other hand, it struck us in that engagement that it's easy to miss the "relationship forest" for the "technology trees." That is, we can focus so much on the technical capacity of such products that we miss the other aspects of building a winning system.

So much of that excellence is in organizational integrity, in terms of the leadership ethic that is created and managed and the values that are built in and around the human resource through recruiting, training, and development.

How can any organization look at the customer service transaction as separate and apart from its own systems, its own people, and its own organizational values?

In the example of the construction management firm, we worked not only to understand customer values and desired outcomes, but the behaviors that were necessary to create them. That's why, in the reserve military unit example, we realized that organizational culture is an artifact of behaviors, which in turn are created by the interaction between leadership and the human resource.

Efficacy in Outcomes

In our Syntonics model, we use two measures of efficacy, or effectiveness, to evaluate our success.

First is a measurement against our larger business objective. That is, did we achieve the business result — e.g., more sales, higher margins, higher customer satisfaction, repeat sales — that we set out to achieve? After all, that is the goal we are working to reach.

Second is a measurement against our strategy and tactics. That is, did we accomplish the intermediate behavioral result — e.g., awareness, lead generation — that we set out to achieve, enroute to the larger business objective?

In building a learning organization, it's important to distinguish between these two results, since it's possible to achieve one without achieving the other.

Let us Know How it Works

There you have it, our approach using our branded Syntonics Relationship Management® strategic planning process to build winning customer interactions.

What more of a blessing can life give any one of us than to be a part of creating a "rising tide that floats all boats," that is, to design the strategies and systems that inspire the desired behaviors that are part of a win-win calculus for our clients, and for their customers and clients?

I'm an old MidWestern boy, born and raised on an Illinois farm, and later nearby in town, where each person knew virtually everyone else. My high school was so small that we had only 100 students, and my 1965 graduating class had 24. I joke that our town had both City Limits signs on the same post!

That environment produced an authenticity based on transparency. In a small town, no one, over the long term, could have successfully masqueraded herself or himself as something other than what she or he was.

Trust was the by-product of that environment, but ultimately it was more than that. Trust was the social glue that held the society together. It was intrinsic to Hume, Illinois, and to a thousand other small towns like it, that enjoyed a homogeneity in known and shared values.

That is not our society today.

As a result, our challenge today is to design and create systems that in part mimic that society of Hume, by creating an atmosphere of knowledge and trust in order to achieve those win-win outcomes.

It's work that we love, and we hope that you've learned something that will help you succeed.

ABOUT SAM WALTZ

*S*ome people know Sam Waltz as a business problem-solving strategist. Others know him as an executive coach and counselor. Others know him as a popular motivational speaker and writer. And just about all of them call him friend, cheerleader and confidante. Known as a coach and counselor to governors, senators, corporate CEOs, and entrepreneurs — and our next generation's rising stars! A native of east central Illinois farm country, he has lived in Delaware since 1975. Sam is a former political reporter, senior DuPont PR executive, and CEO and chairman of the board of the Public Relations Society of America (PRSA). A Vietnam-era veteran who worked in US Army Intelligence, Sam Waltz holds BS and MS degrees from the University of Illinois. His doctoral coursework in public policy was done at the University of Delaware. He is a co-author of Thriving in the Midst of Change.

Contact Information:
Sam Waltz
Atlantic Leadership Institiute
P.O. Drawer 3798
3920 Kennett Pike, Greenville Station
Wilmington, DE 19807-0798
Phone: (302) 777-4774
Fax: (302) 777-4775
E-mail: Sam Waltz@SamWaltz.com
Website: www.Atlantic Leadership.com
www.SamWaltz.com

RESOURCE LISTING

Jae Pierce-Baba
LipShtick Productions
12206 Ridgepoint
Wichita, KS 56235
Phone: (316) 946-0422
Fax: (316) 946-0840
E-mail: jae@jaepierce-baba.com
Website: www.jaepierce-baba.com

Denise S. Bennett
Coaching Visions, LLC
6300-138 Creedmoor Road, #330
Raleigh, NC 27612
Phone: (919) 783-6470
Fax: (919) 783-7663
E-mail:dsb@coachingvisions.net
Website:www.coachingvisions.net

Michael Connor
Creative Transitions
8 Nauset Road
Brockton, MA 02301
Phone: (508) 584-9062
Fax: (508) 580-6466
E-mail: MC@ThriveOnChange.com
Website:www.ThriveOnChange.com

Steve Coscia
Coscia Communications Inc.
1605 Melrose Avenue
Havertown, PA 19083
Phone: (610) 853-9836
Fax: (610) 853-1657
E-mail: steve@coscia.com
Website: www.coscia.com

Linda C. Drake
TCIM Services, Inc.
1011 Centre Road
Wilmington, DE 19805
Phone: (302) 633-3028
Fax: (302) 633-3270
Website: www.tcim.com

Cathy Emma
Voice Power In Business
E-mail: cathy@cathyemma.com
Website: www.cathyemma.com

Paul Johnson
Panache and Systems
149 Azalea Chase Drive
Suwanee, GA 30024
Phone: (770) 271-7719
Fax: (770) 271-7493
E-mail: paul.j@panache-yes.com
Website: www.panache-yes.com

John Kennedy
Kennedy Consulting
2634 Old Washington Road
Westminster, MD 21157
Phone: (410) 751-8838
Fax: (410) 751-9419
E-mail: john@ishakeitup.com
Website: www.ishakeitup.com

Carol A. Kivler
Kivler Communications
8 Hart Court
Titusville, NJ 08560
Phone: (609) 737-8157
Fax: (609) 737-8812
E-mail: kivlercom@worldnet.att.net
Website: www.kivlercom.com

Marian Madonia
Madonia Communications Int'l
4741 Central Street, #115
Kansas City, MO 64112
Phone: (816) 237-8700
E-mail: Marian@MarianMotivates.com
Website: www.MarianMotivates.com

Frank Polkowski
NonProfit & Management
  Consultants
6342 Pin Cherry Court
East Amherst, NY 14051
Phone: (716) 741-7403
Toll Free: (800) 610-6564
Fax: (716) 741-9735
E-mail: FCP@aol.com

Ron Rael
549-227th Lane, NE
Sammamish, WA 98074-7141
Phone: (425) 898-8072
Fax: (425) 898-8902
E-mail: Ron@ronrael.com
Website: www.RonRael.com

Edie Raether
Performance PLUS
4717 Ridge Water Court
Holly Springs, NC 27540
Phone: (919) 557-7900
Fax: (919) 557-7999
E-mail: edie@raether.com
Website: www.raether.com

Debra Schmidt
Spectrum Consulting Group Inc.
P.O. Box 170954
Milwaukee, WI 53217-8086
Phone: (414) 964-3872
Fax: (414) 967-0875
E-mail: Deb@TheLoyaltyBuilder.com
Website: www.TheLoyaltyBuilder.com

Doug Smart
Doug Smart Seminars
P.O. Box 768024
Roswell, GA 30076
Toll Free: (800) 299-3737
Phone: (770) 587-9784
Fax: (770) 587-1050
E-mail: Doug@DougSmart.Seminars
Website: www.DougSmart.com

Dave Timmons
Extreme Leadership Solutions
14910 N. Dale Mabry Highway
P.O. Box 340025
Tampa, FL 33694-0025
Phone: (813) 792-9829
Fax: (813) 792-9810
E-mail: Dave@DaveTimmons.com
Website: www.DaveTimmons.com

Pat Veal
E-mail: PVeal1@bellsouth.net

Sam Waltz
Atlantic Leadership Institiute
P.O. Drawer 3798
3920 Kennett Pike, Greenville Station
Wilmington, DE 19807-0798
Phone: (302) 777-4774
Fax: (302) 777-4775
E-mail: Sam Waltz@SamWaltz.com
Website: www.Atlantic Leadership.com
          www.SamWaltz.com

Bobbe White
Try Laughter! Inc.
1313 South 29th Street
Quincy IL 62301
Phone/Fax: (217) 222-1852
Toll Free: (888) 836-0051
E-mail: Bobbe@TryLaughter.com
Website: www.trylaughter.com

Patti Wood
2312 Hunting Valley Drive
Decatur, GA 30033
Phone: (404) 371-8228
E-mail: Pattiwood@PattiWood.com
Website: www.PattiWood.com
          www.TheBodyLanguageLady.com

NOTES

NOTES

NOTES

NOTES

NOTES